THE HIJACKED CONSCIENCE

An Informed and Compassionate Response to Religious Scrupulosity

DEBRA PECK

Copyright © 2023 by Author and SacraSage Press

All rights reserved. This book or any portion thereof may not be reproduced or used in any manner whatsoever without the express written permission of the publisher except for the use of brief quotations in a book review or scholarly journal.

Print ISBN 978-1-948609-81-4
Ebook ISBN 978-1-948609-82-1

Printed in the United States of America

Library of Congress Cataloguing-in-Publication Data

The Hijacked Conscience: An Informed and Compassionate Response to Religious Scrupulosity / Debra Peck

*To Norman Peck,
my wonderful husband who has patiently
and unwaveringly supported and loved me.
I am grateful for how you have believed in me
and seen in me more than I have seen in myself.
You have my love forever.*

Table of Contents

Foreword xv

Introduction. 1

Part I: The Importance of Understanding Religious Scrupulosity

Chapter 1: Scrupulosity: The Doubting Disease 7

Chapter 2: The Downward Spiral of Scrupulosity 21

Chapter 3: The Difficulty of Seeking and
Receiving Help. 37

Part II: Three Challenges Inherent to Scrupulosity

Chapter 4: Challenge #1: Drowning In Shame 53

Chapter 5: Challenge #2: You Are What You Think. 67

Chapter 6: Challenge #3: The Idol of Certainty. 83

Part III: Helps and Hindrances to Healing from Scrupulosity

Chapter 7: The Call to Bind Up the Brokenhearted. 99

Chapter 8: The Difficulty with Politics, Pandemics, and Preaching. 115

Chapter 9: Hope from a Rewritten Story. 133

Chapter 10: The Continuing Blessing of Healing 151

Appendix 159

References 161

*Unless otherwise noted, all Scripture is from the New International Version of the Bible.

Endorsements for
The Hijacked Conscience by Debra Peck

"Debra Peck offers an important pastoral resource with The Hijacked Conscience. Throughout my own forty years of pastoral ministry, I have regularly encountered the kind of person Debra describes, from her personal testimony and the testimony of others. Although I sought to offer faithful and wise pastoral care to persons suffering 'Scrupulosity,' I did not possess the conceptual framework nor the language to counsel my people who may have been suffering with 'Religious Scrupulosity Obsessive Compulsive Disorder.'

Debra combines personal narrative, solid theological reflection, and clinical awareness to provide a substantive framework to guide the response of pastors and others who seek to care for persons suffering a 'hijacked' conscience. I commend this crucial resource for pastors."

Rev. Jeren Rowell, Ed.D.
President and Professor of Pastoral Ministry
Nazarene Theological Seminary
Kansas City, Missouri

"Religious scrupulosity is a type of OCD that often hides in plain sight in churches, Sunday schools, and within religious families. It often goes unidentified or mistreated by clergy, teachers, and parents alike, sometimes leading sufferers to struggle mightily with the very institution (religion) that is meant to engender a sense of faith and peace in an otherwise uncertain world. Using her own personal experience with scrupulosity and the latest psychological science, Debra Peck helps her readers identify and understand this perplexing problem. Through its clear, thoughtful, and practical writing, 'The Hijacked Conscious' reveals the factors that unwittingly contribute to scrupulosity, as well as how these factors can be reversed to break free from its grip. Full of many insights, this terrific book is a must read for clergy, as well as for family members of those affected by scrupulosity."

Jonathan Abramowitz, PH.D.
Professor of Psychology and Neuroscience at the University of North Carolina (UNC) at Chapel Hill, internationally recognized researcher into OCD, and author of *Getting Over OCD*.

"This is a much-needed book on the often-neglected and little-understood topic of Religious Scrupulosity Obsessive Compulsive Disorder with which the author has struggled throughout her life. In her bid to enable readers to understand how perverse and detrimental to health and spirituality this condition can be she courageously shares her own story of living with this disorder. While noting that this may well be a lifelong condition encouragingly there has been healing for her, especially through life-changing encounters with God and reparative work with a spiritual director although she acknowledges that help from others frequently results in increased obsessive compulsions for those seeking relief from this disorder. I thoroughly recommend this publication to sufferers, pastors, church leaders as well as mental health professionals, and all those who encounter and seek to help those with Religious Scrupulosity Obsessive Compulsive Disorder."

Dr. Gill Harvey
Therapeutic Counsellor/Psychotherapist,
Supervisor, Researcher & Trainer
Registered BACP (Senior Accredited),
ACC (Accredited)

"Before meeting Debra a few years ago, I had never heard of Religious Scrupulosity OCD. While witnessing her journey to greater understanding and health, I have not only encountered others sharing her sufferings but—having grown up in a Holiness Tradition—I can think of many others who struggled with the same burdens without knowing how to name it or find healing. Debra's book *The Hijacked Conscience* is a thoughtful, personal, and helpful resource for those who share a similar emotional makeup to Debra. However, it is also a critically important guide for those of us who regularly invite people to pursue the holy life to be aware when our words, actions, and attitudes cease to become good news for people and instead become an impossible burden to carry; leading people further away rather than closer to God. I'm so thankful for the ways Debra's honest journey and committed research has reshaped my own preaching and ministry."

Dr. Scott Daniels
Senior Pastor - Nampa College Church

"Peck has written a remarkable insider's account and incisive exposition of the intrusive, oppressive, and often paralyzing nature of scrupulosity (religio-spiritual OCD) here. Her book is a gift of tremendous solidarity to those burdened by this incredibly distressing condition and an excellent resource for anyone who wants to helpfully support or spiritually minister to sufferers rather than inadvertently serve to sustain and amplify their burden. In fact, much like churches, ministries, and leaders that fail to be trauma-informed, those who lack awareness of the nature and spiritual impacts of scrupulosity can be similarly more likely to 'tie up heavy burdens and lay them on people's shoulders,' as Jesus prophetically stated of the scribes and Pharisees (or religious leaders) during his own ministry. If Jesus came to 'set the captives free' and wants to use the church to help do so, then I'd say The Hijacked Conscience is a valuable contribution to that liberation. Highly recommended!"

Shane Moe, MA, MDiv, LMFT
Therapist, Certified EMDR Clinician and Consultant

"Through transparent recounting of a lifelong personal struggle, Deb Peck deftly pulls back the curtain on Religious Scrupulosity, a variety of OCD (Obsessive-Compulsive Disorder) sometimes overlooked by those in the helping professions. This heart-wrenching narrative brought to mind hospice patients I've encountered at end-of-life, seeking the assurance of salvation but finding it impossible to believe themselves worthy of God's love and grace. Both well-researched and down-to-earth, *The Highjacked Conscience* effectively points the way to freedom from destructive and incessant self-criticism."

Rev. Gregory Crofford, Ph.D.
Hospice Chaplain
Pittsburgh, Pennsylvania

"Gloriously truthful. Refreshing. Insightful. As a fellow sufferer of scrupulosity, I was profoundly impacted by the grace and grit woven throughout Peck's narrative. Her words reached places in my own soul with an unparalleled reflectivity—validating my own experiences through a lens of authenticity and compassion like no one else has ever done. Through her candid and courageous reflections, Peck captures the heart of a raw and lonely struggle so many of us have had to endure on our own. This book cracks open that loneliness through its vulnerability, revealing the truth down to the details and offering a tangible hope that healing truly can happen. Part memoir, part education, and pure enlightenment, 'The Hijacked Conscience' will open the eyes of anyone who is willing to approach it."

El
diagnosed with Religious Scrupulosity OCD

Foreword

The term "suffering saint" has been heard less often in the church during recent years, but for past generations, it indicated ways Christians were persecuted or harmed in this evil world. Many of the saints were comforted by saying, "We are just passing through—our home is in Heaven." Suffering was viewed as part of life and handed a badge of spirituality. In truth, much of the suffering was needless and made worse by church teachings.

Inward suffering was either ignored or attributed to a lack of spirituality. No one considered that it was possible to suffer because of a deep desire to follow God and every teaching the church offered. It was this overzealous emphasis on doing everything to please God—and the church—that became fertile ground for *The Hijacked Conscience* and Debra's story of suffering.

Debra Peck and I met in 2020 when we spoke at a Wesleyan theology conference on disability in the church. My topic was the impact of trauma; her presentation was on Religious Scrupulosity—something I was sure I had heard of but knew little about. Unfortunately, the first offering of our sessions was at the same time, but Debra introduced herself when she attended my repeat session and offered to share her speaker notes. What I read made so much sense! I realized that this was likely far more common than most imagined. Those initial notes were the foundation for *The Hijacked Conscience: An Informed and Compassionate Response to Religious Scrupulosity*.

During the two years since our initial meeting, I have followed along as Debra developed the content and vulnerably shared her story. As her childhood and adult story unfolded on the documents she shared with me, I realized that her desire to help others who might be suffering from Religious Scrupulosity was possibly one of the most courageous efforts I had seen in my lifetime. The basis of scrupulosity is the fear of doing something wrong. In Religious Scrupulosity, the burden of displeasing God can be nearly impossible to bear. For any who have suffered trauma, sharing their story is often necessary to obtain freedom—and a terrifying choice. *The Hijacked Conscience* is not only a tribute to Debra's hard work to heal, the research to thoroughly understand scrupulosity, but also the power of those who heal and then courageously work to bring help to others.

I hope that ministry leaders will read *The Hijacked Conscience* and add the wisdom shared in these pages to their trauma-responsive practices. A hallmark of trauma-responsive churches is the honor given to the sacred stories of those who suffered and were often misjudged by those who lacked understanding. Let Debra's story, courage, and wisdom be your guide in alleviating the pain of those who suffer.

—**Janyne McConnaughey, Ph.D.**; Author, *Trauma in the Pews: The Impact on Faith and Spiritual Practices*

Introduction

Religious Scrupulosity Obsessive Compulsive Disorder is not generally one of the first things to pop into one's mind when one thinks about mental illnesses. In fact, few people I have encountered throughout my life have heard of it. Ironically, though, as soon as I start describing it, people often recognize themselves or someone they know in the description.

"Hijacked" is an apt term for what happens in the brain of a person with Religious Scrupulosity OCD. Generally speaking, hijack means to take over by force, to take over and change direction, or to take over for a different purpose. It can also mean to take captive. Scrupulosity does just that, forcefully taking over the good, healthy, helpful conscience of a person and holding it captive for other purposes. Often mistaken as being "just overly conscientious," Scrupulosity is instead relentless and unmerciful in its assault on a person's spiritual and religious experiences and, by extension, every aspect of that person's life.

Eight years ago, after nearly forty years of suffering, I discovered I have Religious Scrupulosity Obsessive Compulsive Disorder. Because Scrupulosity was not well known or recognized, from childhood on, I had thought I had spiritual issues and was not trying hard enough or had not figured out what it was that God wanted from me, even though I was trying to live as conscientiously as I possibly could. Thinking it was a spiritual issue, I naturally sought out the help of pastors and other religious leaders, but because none of them were familiar with Scrupulosity, they were unable to help me and, in some instances, caused further harm in their efforts to help. Scrupulosity completely took over my life and left me unable to enjoy my relationship with God, and nearly incapacitated me with its demands of a level of perfection I could never attain.

Since discovering I have Religious Scrupulosity OCD and experiencing healing mentally, emotionally, and spiritually, I have been motivated to share my experiences with those who may also be suffering from Scrupulosity, as well as to inform and educate pastors, other religious leaders, and anyone who might be mentoring someone with Scrupulosity about this debilitating mental illness. Although it has been disheartening to hear how few have heard of Scrupulosity, it has also been rewarding to hear from dear friends and strangers alike who recognize their own struggles in my story and now have hope for healing. As one friend put it, "I didn't know [what I was experiencing] had a name!" Pastors and other religious leaders have also shared their recognition of those in their congregation, either currently or in the past, who likely had or have Scrupulosity, and their appreciation for my story and the resources for how to more effectively minister to those who struggle.

Religious Scrupulosity OCD is more common than is generally recognized. With proper education, pastors and other religious leaders have an opportunity to make a significant difference in the lives of those who deal with it. If just one of my pastors or Sunday school teachers had known about Religious Scrupulosity OCD, I believe my life would have been much different, and I would have been spared years of intense spiritual and mental suffering. I hope that as pastors, Sunday school teachers, and other leaders within the church learn about Religious Scrupulosity OCD, they will be able to minister effectively to those who suffer.

In the pages of this book, I will help the reader understand what Religious Scrupulosity Obsessive-Compulsive Disorder is, how it can be identified in ministry settings, as well as offer practical steps for helping someone you may suspect has Religious Scrupulosity OCD. My own story will be interwoven throughout as a backdrop illustrating what I am attempting to convey. Pastors, Sunday School teachers, and other leaders who are educated and equipped to deal with Religious Scrupulosity OCD have a chance to make a significant difference in the lives of those who struggle with this soul-crushing condition.

This book is also for those who struggle with a "hijacked conscience" and who see their own stories reflected in my story. Recognizing I had Scrupulosity was eye-opening for me and helped me start the process of breaking free from it. My hope is that, as you read, you will also find the courage to find effective treatment, as well as help educate your pastors and others about Scrupulosity.

This book is broken up into three sections. Part one covers how to recognize Scrupulosity and why it is important to understand what it is. Part two covers some of the particular challenges those with Scrupulosity face. Part three covers how healing from Scrupulosity can be helped or hindered by those around the individual with Scrupulosity. At the end, an appendix will provide a list of further resources.

*Note on terms: There are several ways to refer to Religious Scrupulosity Obsessive-Compulsive Disorder, and throughout the book, I use them somewhat interchangeably. Most often, I use Scrupulosity OCD or just Scrupulosity. When I want to emphasize the religious aspect, I include Religious, and when I want to emphasize that it is a mental illness, I include OCD. In addition, I use the abbreviation RSOCD.

Disclaimer: This book is not intended to diagnose or act as a substitute or replacement for the professional services of a physician or mental health provider who is trained to recognize and treat anxiety disorders or other mental health issues. If you or a loved one are suffering from severe anxiety, depression, or other mental health concerns, please talk to your doctor or other health professional.

Part I

The Importance of Understanding Religious Scrupulosity

Chapter 1

Scrupulosity: The Doubting Disease

The stage was set. I stood frozen, panic rising, heart racing as I tried to will my hands to do what my mind was screaming not to. The ordinariness of my surroundings belied the seriousness of the situation. Those next few moments could decide my eternal destiny. After several long minutes of my mind sifting through the possibilities, I turned away, unable to complete the task. My husband reached out to do what I did not dare to do. With the clunk of the can of green beans in the grocery cart, we moved on down the aisle toward the next potential soul-damning choice.

Looking back, I am astonished that a seemingly easy decision—which can of green beans to buy—could lead to such panic, yet I remember when every decision was like that. I lived as if each choice I made throughout the day, each task I accomplished, and every thought that went through my head could send me to hell. I feared sinning and worried that I either had sinned or might sin or that I was not living a holy enough life. Pastors and other religious leaders were poorly trained to deal with the depth of my anguish and often blamed me for not trying hard enough or else completely dismissed my concerns as just being overly conscientious. Both of those approaches were inadequate for what I was actually dealing with, Religious Scrupulosity Obsessive-Compulsive Disorder.

By way of introduction to our topic, I want you to pretend for a few minutes that you are my pastor. You know me to be a conscientious Christian, faithful in my church attendance, and living out my faith in a holy and consistent way. Most importantly, of course, I am a great tither! I have made an appointment to see you and am now sitting in your office. I want you to think about what you would say to me in response to the following concerns:

- "Pastor, I don't know what to do! On Sunday, you preached that I could 'know that I know that I know that I'm saved,' but I don't know! What's wrong with me?"

- "How do I know if I've committed the unpardonable sin? I'm so afraid I have. I don't know what I did, but I feel like I might have so displeased God that I can't possibly be saved."

- "I made a vow to God that I wouldn't drink coffee during Lent, but I forgot one day. I've failed God, and now I'm afraid He won't have me back. The Bible says that anyone who puts his hand to the plow and looks back isn't fit for the kingdom."

- "I was at the gas station yesterday, and I saw a person there who obviously needed Jesus. I know I should have gone over and talked to her, but I was in a hurry. Now I can't get it out of my mind that I disobeyed God. If this woman dies without knowing God and goes to hell, it's my fault!"

- "I'm so ashamed to admit it, but when I try to read my Bible, I have blasphemous thoughts about God. The Bible says, 'As a man thinks in his heart, so is he.' I'm so afraid that I'm evil or demon-possessed."

- "How do I know if I was really sincere when I asked God to forgive me? I have asked Jesus into my heart so many times, but He just won't come in. I beg Him to 'purge me with hyssop, and I will be clean, wash me, and I will be whiter than snow,' but I still feel so unclean and unforgiven. Maybe I'm not being sincere."

- "At work last week, our boss had a meeting with all the employees and said that someone has been stealing from some of the residents in the nursing home. I felt so guilty! I'm afraid I've been stealing and don't know it!"

- "I haven't been able to pray in months. Every time I try, I have sexual thoughts about God. I don't want to feel that way about the God I love, so I can't pray anymore. But how can I be a Christian if I don't pray?"

These questions and a thousand different variations on a theme are things with which a person with Religious Scrupulosity Obsessive-Compulsive Disorder will struggle. How do you answer them? What do you say that will bring them comfort and relief? As a person who has dealt with Scrupulosity OCD for most of my life, I have asked many of these questions. Here are a few of the answers I and others have received:

- "Maybe you are harboring some secret sin that you need to confess to God."
- "God is faithful, so if your relationship with God is suffering, the problem is you."
- "If you feel far from God, you moved, not God!"
- "You just need to pray for more faith."
- "You are carnal. You need to really sell out to God and get sanctified."
- "You need to pray more, read your Bible more, fast more ... more ... more ... more."
- "You are letting Satan confuse you."
- "You need to show God that you mean business, that you are serious about serving Him."
- "God has not given you a spirit of fear, so if you're fearful, you're not trusting God."
- "God may be testing your faith. It's in the desert we learn to trust."
- "The Bible says to be anxious about nothing, so you need to stop letting your anxiety control you. Give it to God!"

Answers like these do little to help a person who is struggling. Most of them are guilt-inducing and bypass the very real pain and confusion a person experiencing those questions is dealing with. In addition, those answers assume the person is not already doing their best to live for God. Often this is not the case. Those types of answers can cause further harm to a person already struggling.

There is another approach many of us have experienced, as well. Rooted in giving assurance to the sufferer, here are some typical answers:

- "Of course, you're saved! There's no doubt in my mind."
- "If you're worried you committed the unpardonable sin, you know you haven't."
- "You have nothing to worry about! You are such a faithful servant of God."
- "I wish everyone in my congregation was as conscientious as you."
- "When those bad thoughts happen, just quote Scripture or plead the blood of Jesus. You know Jesus met temptation by quoting Scripture."
- "Don't settle for anything less than full assurance. God is faithful."
- "I'll be praying for you that you'll find that assurance."

Would it surprise you to know that these answers may be just as harmful to a person with Scrupulosity OCD as the other set of responses was?

So, what exactly is Religious Scrupulosity Obsessive-Compulsive Disorder? The word comes from the Latin word *scrupulum*, which means a small sharp stone. It evokes the picture of walking with a stone in your shoe. The International OCD Foundation describes it as "A form of Obsessive-Compulsive Disorder (OCD) involving religious or moral obsessions. Scrupulous individuals are overly concerned that something they thought or did might be a sin or other violation of religious or moral doctrine."[1] In simplest terms, people with Scrupulosity OCD see sin where there is none.

Scrupulosity OCD was first identified in the 1600s by priests in monasteries. Abbots noticed that some monks would read Scripture, pray, attend confession, and do acts of penance far beyond what was required. These monks would often beat themselves for minor infractions, fast for extended amounts of time, or crawl on their knees until they were bloody.

Those who suffer from Scrupulosity usually have an overly sensitive moral conscience which causes their faith to be experienced as anxiety and fear instead of as peace. The French call it "the doubting disease." People with Scrupulosity hold themselves to a rigorous level of spirituality and practice, not out of love or even out of obligation, but out of deep-seated fear and anxiety that not doing so imperils their eternal soul.

Like all forms of Obsessive-Compulsive Disorder, Scrupulosity is marked by unwanted and intrusive thoughts (obsessions), overwhelming anxiety that demands resolution, and either outward or internal rituals (compulsions) that relieve the anxiety for a time. Perhaps the easiest way to explain it is to use an example we are probably all familiar with, germ obsession. Some people with OCD who become obsessed with germs will have a thought that maybe they touched something with germs on it. This may or may not be true, but the thought is there.

---

1. https://iocdf.org/wp-content/uploads/2014/10/IOCDF-Scrupulosity-Fact-Sheet.pdf

In response, they start experiencing extreme anxiety. "What if I touched something someone who has the flu touched? It's on my hands now! What if I get the flu? People die from the flu. I could die!!" This anxiety pushes them toward a solution—washing their hands. When they wash their hands, the anxiety is dealt with, and they feel better ... until the thought happens again. Because their anxiety is relieved, each time they wash their hands, *they reinforce the seriousness and rightness of the anxiety and give credence to it*, thus making the thought occur more and more often, requiring more frequent hand-washing. Many with this type of Obsessive-Compulsive Disorder avoid situations that might result in germs on their hands, like shaking hands or touching surfaces, and in severe cases, they avoid going out into public at all.

With Religious Scrupulosity OCD, the originating thought (the "germ") is a fear of sinning or failing to do religious duties correctly. For example, a person with Scrupulosity may decide to read the Bible all the way through in a year. (Often, this is due to receiving the message that reading the Bible is really, really important, and good Christians will read the whole Bible.) As they make their way through the book of Numbers, they find their mind wandering as they read all the lists of names. The thought crosses their mind, "I think I might have skipped a word." So, they go back and reread the verse, but they think they still may have skipped a word, so they go back and read again ... and again ... and again. They are convinced: "If I don't read every word, then I'm lying if I say I've read the Bible all the way through." Anxiety starts to build. Another thought crosses their mind, "Why am I skipping words? Every word in the Bible is important! I'm being disrespectful if I don't read every word. What's wrong with me? Is the devil trying to make me miss words so I won't be able to obey God? Maybe I'm not a Christian after all." So, the person feels compelled (compulsion) to painstakingly go back and read every word—every impossible-to-pronounce name—pausing appropriately at every comma. Their anxiety is relieved ... until they "miss" a word again. The fact that their anxiety is relieved by doing the compulsion reinforces that it indeed was a serious issue. For many people with Scrupulosity OCD, reading the Bible becomes a nearly impossible task, and they avoid it altogether. This, of course, raises another anxiety. How can I be a Christian if I do not read the Bible? And so, the cycle goes.

For a person with Scrupulosity OCD, there are no gray areas. There is black or white; sinful or not sinful; moral or immoral; right or wrong. For every decision, there is only one right answer, so making the most straightforward choices can be overwhelming because, for instance, if I choose the wrong can of green beans at the grocery store, I may be following my sinful desires instead of my holy desires. Which socks I choose to wear today may decide my eternal destiny. Everything becomes a moral issue. As you can imagine, this can be quite paralyzing.

For those from a Wesleyan-holiness position which emphasizes that the heart can be completely cleansed from sin and living a sin-free life is the expectation of those who are "sanctified," this can be especially debilitating. In addition, John Wesley's teaching on the assurance of the believer to "know that they know that they know they are saved"—when improperly understood—seems unattainable for sufferers of Scrupulosity, setting them up for intense self-doubt and fear that they have not really given Jesus lordship in their lives. Poorly understood doctrines—either because of inadequate or abusive teachings by church leaders or poor understanding on the part of the individual—can become sources for debilitating obsessions.

Common Obsessions of Scrupulosity OCD

While the list of obsessions associated with Scrupulosity OCD is as varied as the people who suffer from it, several themes emerge as common among them. Some obsessive intrusive thoughts a person with scrupulosity might have include:

- Frequently occurring thoughts or fears about being sinful. Thoughts of sinning—far beyond normal temptation—plague people with RSOCD. Unwanted thoughts such as stealing something in a store, molesting a child, cheating on a test, lying, etc., will torment their thoughts even though those are things the individual has no desire to do and has never done.

- Ruminating (turning over and over in their mind) past mistakes, failures, actual sins, and the possibility of having sinned. There is a constant need to scrutinize every thought and conversation to check for sin and to mentally relive those moments "correctly."

- Overwhelming fear of committing blasphemy. For some, intrusive blasphemous thoughts will enter their minds, and they become afraid to speak. They fear blaspheming the Holy Spirit and thus damning themselves to hell. Many will experience this during prayer, leading to an inability to pray because they fear accidentally blaspheming God.

- Intense focus on being religiously and morally perfect. Every moment of their lives must be perfectly lived; every little detail of their existence must be holy.

- Unwanted and intrusive sexual thoughts about God, Jesus, or a religious leader. These are extremely common and cause significant mental distress, especially considering Jesus' teaching that a man who lusts after a person in their heart (thoughts) is already committing adultery.

- Repetitive thoughts of eternal damnation and preoccupation with the fear they have committed the "unpardonable sin" or "crossed the deadline" and cannot be saved.

- Overwhelming fear and anxiety that a loved one is going to go to hell. Along with this fear, obsessive thoughts about the need to evangelize people, even strangers, plague them.

- Food-related obsessions related to a misunderstanding of the body being "the temple of the Holy Spirit." This often includes excessive fasting or avoidance of certain food groups—especially sugar or foods deemed unhealthy.

- Fear of the loss of impulse control, such as the fear that one might suddenly jump off a cliff if one stands too close to the edge. (Different from the fear of falling, it is the fear that one will lose control of their mind and jump on purpose.)

For a person with Scrupulosity OCD, there is no such thing as "just a thought." For instance, many, many people driving along in a car will have the thought cross their mind that they might veer off the road and hit a tree. Most people can dismiss that thought as a stray thought, recognizing that our brains are aware that people sometimes do drive off the road into things. It does not mean they will. People with Scrupulosity think that if the thought is there, it is what they want to do. If it is what they want to do, then they are evil. It is important to understand that with Scrupulosity OCD, it is not the *thought* that is the problem—we all have stray thoughts—it is the *anxiety* the thought produces. Obsessive-Compulsive Disorder is not a thought disorder; it is an anxiety disorder.

Common Compulsions of Scrupulosity OCD

Individuals with Religious Scrupulosity OCD will develop compulsions to "neutralize" the guilt and anxiety caused by their obsessive thoughts. Some common compulsions include:

- Repeatedly confessing the same sins to those in religious authority (pastor, Sunday School teacher, etc.), or children confessing the same instances of disobedience to parents. Many times, these confessions happen over and over within the same day or night in order for the person to make sure they have properly confessed and can receive forgiveness.

- Avoiding particular objects which are associated with immorality. Included in this would be the inability to tolerate foul language, not looking through a sales paper for fear there could be a person dressed in a way that would trigger an immoral thought, and even avoiding religious icons or symbols which they think could lead to blasphemous or sexual thoughts.

- Out of proportion or excessive reading of religious texts and spending extended amounts of time in prayer, both to show faithfulness to God and to make sure they are correctly fulfilling their religious duties.

- Seeking reassurance from others that one has not sinned or been immoral.

- Avoidance of religious services, traditions, or objects due to fears of being unworthy or sinful. Refusing to participate in the Eucharist is a common one because of the fear of "eating unworthily to their own damnation (1 Corinthians 11:27 KJV)."

- Excessive repetition of specific verses of Scripture or certain religious songs to ward off bad thoughts.

- Physically beating oneself to make amends for sins or to show God how seriously they take their sinfulness.

Religious Scrupulosity OCD is an equal-opportunity mental illness. All religions have people who are affected by it. There is even a type of Scrupulosity called Moral Scrupulosity OCD which affects people who are not religious. Not surprisingly, the manifestations of Scrupulosity OCD vary with the religious beliefs of a person. For instance, a Muslim would experience blasphemous thoughts about Mohammed, whereas a Christian would not. A Jew might excessively read the Torah, whereas a Latter-Day Saint would read the Book of Mormon. A Catholic may be obsessed with genuflecting correctly or praying the Lord's Prayer a certain number of times. Whatever the important tenets of each religion, those are the areas where Scrupulosity OCD will manifest itself.

There is speculation that several very well-known religious people throughout history suffered from Scrupulosity, including John Bunyan, Saint Ignatius of Loyola, and quite likely Martin Luther. Each of these wrote about their experiences with conscientiousness. There has also been speculation that John Wesley was driven by intense scrupulosity.

Left untreated, Scrupulosity OCD can leave a person nearly incapacitated. The rituals (compulsions) to deal with the anxiety caused by Scrupulosity can claim ever-increasing portions of a person's day, leaving them unable to function in their other responsibilities such as work and family. It also greatly impacts their relationships with others, especially pastors and other religious leaders as the need for confession and reassurance becomes more frequent. Ultimately, it can also lead to more severe issues like self-harm.

If you are reading this and perhaps recognize yourself in the descriptions of Scrupulosity, then you no doubt see both the need to understand more about yourself and your struggles, as well as the powerful help it can be for those around you to understand what you are experiencing. So many of us have borne shame and even abuse at the hands of religious leaders who had no understanding of the devastation Scrupulosity has caused in our spiritual lives and relationship with God. When I discovered I had Religious Scrupulosity Obsessive-Compulsive Disorder, it was the beginning of my journey to freedom, and that is my hope for you, as well.

If you do not personally suffer from Scrupulosity, you might be thinking, "Why does any of this matter to me? I'm not a psychologist!" If you think about how Scrupulosity presents itself, though, you will have a clue as to why it should matter to you. Scrupulosity presents as a *spiritual* problem. To whom do you take a spiritual issue? You take them to your pastor, Sunday School teacher, or another trusted spiritual leader. Scrupulosity generally does not appear first in a counselor's office; it shows up in the pastor's office. It stands to reason, then, that if spiritual leaders and mentors are not trained to recognize it, they can do more harm to the person they are trying to help. It is my hope that as you learn about how Religious Scrupulosity OCD affects those to whom you minister, you will be able to come alongside the person suffering and help guide them towards healing and hope.

Chapter 2
The Downward Spiral of Scrupulosity

"McDonald's." My mind acknowledged reading the word even as my conscience was filled with guilt and fear for having done so. Reading anything secular on "the Sabbath" was forbidden, but I had inadvertently allowed my eyes to glance out the window at the brightly colored sign. Quickly pushing aside the fear that I could get in a car accident and die before asking forgiveness, I sent up my customary prayer, "Purge me with hyssop, and I will be clean. Wash me, and I will be whiter than snow." Begging God for forgiveness, I rode the rest of the way to church studiously keeping my eyes fixed on my hands clasped in my lap so my sixteen-year-old self would not read something else and risk dying before I had a chance to ask for forgiveness again. Unfortunately, at sixteen, Scrupulosity OCD already had a firm grip on me.

I first began to develop Scrupulosity in my early teens, although the seeds for it were planted much earlier than that. When I was a young child, my family attended an ultra-conservative holiness church. Women wore dresses, did not wear jewelry or cut their hair, did not watch TV, etc. These and a myriad of other written and unwritten rules were considered necessary for holy living. When I was four years old, I gave my heart to Jesus during a Sunday School class. I remember being filled with such love for Jesus and a deep desire to please Him. When I was five, my mom, two siblings, and I left that church and began to attend the Church of the Nazarene. My dad quit attending church altogether, but my other siblings and most of my dad's relatives still attended the other church. They began to tell us we were going to go to hell because we were wearing pants, cutting our hair, etc. They even went so far as to tell my siblings and me that our mother was leading us to hell. This was very confusing to me as a young child. I knew I had given my heart to Jesus and loved him, but they said I was still going to hell.

One of the consequences of this for me, personally, was that I was not allowed to develop a healthy self-identity. In order to survive the complicated and confusing world around me, I unconsciously learned to place my identity outside of myself. I became completely dependent on those around me for any sense of identity or worth. The messages mirrored back from my family, my church—and by extension, God—were that I was inadequate, unholy, pitiful, and in desperate need of others to make sure I was the person I needed to be in order to be worthy of God's presence in my life. The things I did, my thoughts, and my feelings also became intricately linked to my identity. Instead of my thoughts, actions, and feelings flowing out of my identity, I viewed my identity as based on those things. Doing was first, instead of being. This lack of personhood, identity, and worth set the stage, I believe, for Scrupulosity to begin to take over my life.

For the next several years, whenever the conservative holiness church would have revivals, we would attend there.

Services at that church were quite emotional. People getting "blessed," shouting, and running the aisles were frequent occurrences. This was equated with the presence of God, and I do believe I experienced the felt presence of God many times in those services. However, because my relatives said I was not a Christian and because they said the only way an unsaved person could experience God's presence was through the conviction of the Holy Spirit, I came to associate God's presence only with conviction. Guilt-inducing statements by the pastors and evangelists just served to further this misunderstanding. For instance, during the music (hymns only, naturally), we were often told, "If you don't feel God's presence, there's something wrong with you!" The opposite of that, of course, was, "If you feel God's presence and you are not saved, you are feeling conviction. Come to the altar and get saved!" Being a conscientious child who truly desired to follow Jesus, I would go to the altar time and time again, thinking I was responding to the conviction of the Holy Spirit.

Emotional and spiritual manipulation was very much a part of that church's way of operating. For instance, an integral part of demonstrating that a person was saved was to raise their hand in praise to God during the singing; and another was standing to testify, "I know I am saved and sanctified, and on my way to heaven." These were not as straightforward as you might think. If you did not raise your hand during singing, then obviously you did not think you were saved, but if you did and those around you did not think you were, then you could practically feel their disapproval and skepticism. In many instances, the pastor or evangelist would talk to you about it and express concern for your soul. For me, again, as a very conscientious child, to begin with, this was difficult to navigate.

Most of the time, I would not raise my hand because I was not completely sure I was saved, but I also knew I loved God very much, and so I felt like I was denying Jesus if I did not raise my hand. Religious services became places where I experienced constant turmoil and self-doubt.

When I was about nine, I was at a tent meeting revival with the other church. When the altar call was given, I knew I was feeling the presence of God. I became concerned that even though I had invited Jesus into my heart, maybe I had not properly asked for forgiveness for my sins, so I went forward to pray to have my sins forgiven. One of my relatives came and began to pray with me as I knelt there. "Debi, tell God you'll quit wearing pants. Tell God you'll quit cutting your hair. Tell God you'll quit watching TV." I remember kneeling there feeling devastated, knowing I would never be able to measure up. I knew I would never be good enough, holy enough; whatever the enough was, I knew I would never get there. I left the altar that night defeated and confused. This was a pivotal point in my young life and one that left lasting scars.

For the next couple of years, I would go back and forth between trying to follow the rules of the conservative church and following the rules of the Nazarene church we attended. When I followed the rules of the conservative church, my dad would tell me I was "brainwashed" and make fun of me, and my Nazarene friends would tell me how unnecessary it was to follow all those rules. When I stopped following those rules and lived by the far-less restrictive rules of the Nazarene church, my other relatives would tell me I was on my way to hell. All I wanted was to love and serve God. It seemed an impossible task. Because as a child, I was dependent on those around me to teach me how to know God's will, I was at their mercy. The need for each side to be "right" trumped the need to protect and help a young struggling child.

When I was about eleven, I decided to prove to God that I was serious about serving God, so I became very diligent about spiritual things. Gleaning from what I had been taught over the years as necessary to serve God, I set up a strict devotional time with a rigid way of reading my Bible. I began to pray in specific ways, repeating things in the same way. Having read the Levitical laws about priests having to be clean before entering the Temple to serve, I would wash before devotional times or religious services. I could not pray unless my body was appropriately clothed—my most personal parts completely covered. No praying in the shower for me! In fact, being naked at all became nearly intolerable for fear that I would accidentally pray while uncovered. The "sinner's prayer" was often on my lips. (Because, as I had been taught, "God won't hear the prayer of a sinner unless it's a prayer for salvation.") At about this same time, a preacher spoke about how the Apostle Paul had "beat his body into submission." So, I added that to my devotional time. I would beat myself to show God I was sorry for my sins and serious about serving God.

Those were dark times. Nothing I did brought the peace with God I so desperately sought. I spiraled down into a deep depression. My thoughts became crowded with fear and anxiety that I would die and go to hell if I did not get this figured out. Even though I loved God and had no desire other than to please Him, I knew I would hear the words, "I never knew you." I began to develop significant phobias surrounding the fear of dying. In the course of an ordinary day, I played out a dozen different ways I could die. I could fall off a bridge and drown in the river—so I became unable to cross bridges by myself. I could get in a car accident and die, so praying the sinner's prayer each time I got in a vehicle became necessary. I might get electrocuted, so no plugging things in, or if I had to, praying first. I might get struck by lightning, so under no circumstances could I go outside or near a window during a storm. Spiders, snakes, bees, and all other insects could elicit full-on panic, which resulted in me avoiding going outside. My fear of heights was so severe that I could barely climb up a short ladder. In addition, I became fearful I would be assaulted. One of the worst fears was of being alone.

Depression and fear almost completely took over my life. I wanted so badly to have the peace with God that was promised to those who were in a relationship with Jesus. The fact that I only had fear and darkness convinced me I really must not be saved, so just before my sixteenth birthday, I left home and moved to Washington State to live with my relatives who were part of the conservative holiness denomination I had attended as a child. I decided I would throw myself entirely into following all their rules so that maybe, finally, I would find God.

It is difficult to describe our family dynamics to those who have not experienced them, but their profound impact on my life is such a significant part of my story that I need to try briefly. My dad was the oldest of six siblings. About ten years before I was born, my grandparents and most of my aunts, uncles, and cousins left the Nazarene church they had attended for many years and began attending the conservative holiness denomination which had sprung up in the area. My dad refused to go with them, but my mom and my older siblings joined them at this new church. My dad quit attending church altogether.

My mom did not agree with the rules imposed by the conservative church, but she tried to follow them, with my dad making fun of her the whole time. Eventually, she arrived at the point where she became convinced that God did not require a person to follow all those rules in order to be saved. As I mentioned earlier, she, along with two of my older siblings and myself, left that church and returned to the Nazarene church. This was an incredibly courageous decision my mom made. She was far away from her own family and trying to raise eight kids under some difficult circumstances. Once her decision was made, though, she stood strong in it, even though it brought the derision and harassment of my dad's family. What neither she nor my dad realized, though, was how the family treated my siblings and me as a result. Perhaps even more significant is the wedge the relatives drove between our parents and us. Because my dad was not attending church, and because my mom was not following the rules of the conservative church, our relatives subtly taught us that our parents were not trustworthy and that we had to defy them if we wanted to be saved. As a child, this was extremely detrimental to my development, leaving me disconnected from that security.

One particular relative held a place of honor and respect in the family and in her church community. To be loved and accepted by this relative was to be loved and accepted by God. Although quite a few of my family members took it upon themselves at different times to try to convince my parents, siblings, and me to "return from our backsliding," it was this relative who exerted the strongest level of pressure on us. Because we were not "following God," she would not allow her children to play with us when they lived near us, and because we had a TV in our house, I do not remember their family ever coming over to visit. After they moved from Idaho to Washington, whenever we went to visit them, we girls had to change into dresses so we were modest enough to play with her children. (This was also at the insistence of another relative whose husband was pastoring the church. She felt they needed to protect their witness in the neighborhood.) While these things were hurtful and, indeed, did great damage to us, I do believe my relatives were trying to follow God the best they knew how. I believe they each suffered from some level of the same sort of scrupulous tendencies as I did.

For me to choose, then, to go live with these relatives was a significant thing. I was convinced that if I lived with this important relative, I would finally be able to figure out my relationship with God and find peace. It probably comes as no surprise that I found more darkness and despair instead of peace.

My relative was unrelenting in her criticism of me and in the subtle ways she undermined my relationship with God. It is beyond the scope of this book to delve into the emotional, mental, and physical abuse that took place while I lived in her home, not to mention the spiritual abuse, but my already mentally and emotionally fragile self was nearly destroyed in that year and a half.

When moving in with these conservative relatives, throwing myself fully into following the rules of the church, and meticulously trying to guard myself against sin did not bring the peace and relationship with God I was so desperately seeking, I began to seek out my pastor and other religious leaders for help. I would talk about how I did not feel like I was saved and my fear that I had somehow committed the unpardonable sin. Mostly I was told I still must not have surrendered to God or that I lacked faith. I was told to read my Bible and pray more. In those rare moments when I would feel close to God, though, I could count on this one relative coming to me "concerned for my soul," and because I looked to her to make sure I was doing okay spiritually, down I would go again. The most compassionate response was from a relative who was my pastor at that time. He anointed me with oil and prayed over me. As you may guess, while compassionate, it still gave credence to the seriousness of my anxieties and contributed to making them worse.

To be fair, my family had no idea of the depth of my depression nor of the obsessive-compulsive issues with which I was struggling. I had no name for them, and churches in the 80s were well behind the power curve in recognizing and treating mental illnesses, especially holiness churches which understood and taught that sanctification completely changed a person. To admit one struggled with the things I was struggling with would have, no doubt, brought condemnation and accusations that I was still "carnal."

It is important to note that during that point in history within more conservative church denominations, strict adherence to rules was not only expected but also highly praised. Persons who were extremely conscientious were held up as model Christians. In addition, I was surrounded by family who took this to extremes, so this seemed "normal" to me. The model of what it meant to be a Christian was nothing short of perfection.

Being unable to "find God" led to a deepening of the depression I had been dealing with for several years until it became almost a felt darkness around me, trapping me down inside a dark tunnel from which I tried to live my life.

After graduating high school, I went to the conservative church denomination's Bible college. The pressure intensified. There was unrelenting preaching about consecration and proving to God that we were sincere. The Scrupulosity intensified to become almost all-consuming. I would go over and over every thought, conversation, and deed I had done to see if I had sinned in any way. My constant prayer from Psalm 51 was, "Purge me with hyssop, and I will be clean. Wash me, and I will be whiter than snow." Many times, I would lie face-down in my dorm's storage closet crying out to God to please accept me. Whenever I tried to read my Bible, though, blasphemous thoughts would bombard my mind. I was afraid to read but also afraid not to read because, I thought, if I don't read my Bible, I'm not really a Christian.

There, too, I sought the advice of pastors and professors and was again told I lacked faith or sincerity. I must be holding out on God. There were exceptions, though, thankfully. One of our Bible professors offered reassurance and compassion to me; her extended grace was a bright light in the darkness, but it was not enough to counter the myriad of other voices.

During this time, I experienced one of the most difficult things of my entire life: I stopped experiencing God's felt presence. In service after service where others were being blessed and experiencing God's presence, God's voice and felt presence were seemingly completely missing from my life. There was no assurance that I was God's child, but neither was there the conviction of the Holy Spirit. I was devastated by this and took it to mean that I must have committed the unpardonable sin and could never be saved. One of my relatives even told me that she no longer felt led by God to pray for me, and so she also believed I could not be saved.

In the middle of my freshman year, not wanting to add to my punishment by continuing to live and commit more sins, I decided that since I was going to hell anyway, I might as well commit suicide and end the agony I was in. I attempted and thankfully failed.[2] Afterward, I continued to beg God to speak to me, to save me, and to bring me peace. I knew the Bible said that those who seek God with their whole hearts will find God, so I continued trying to prove to God that I was sincere in seeking God.

Between my first and second years of college, I took a year off to work and save money for the next year. I stayed with my sister and her family down in New Mexico. By then, my depression was so severe that I could barely function, and the Scrupulosity made it so difficult to read my Bible and pray that I had almost completely stopped. I truly felt as if I was living down in a dark tunnel, that everything I said and did felt disconnected from me by a great distance. Trying to concentrate on what others said and what I was supposed to be doing was like swimming through molasses in January. All my energy went into functioning well enough to hold down a job. I had nothing left beyond that.

During this time, I attended a very small conservative holiness church with my sister's family. The elderly pastor, while legalistic in some regards, had tremendous compassion for me and would tell me often that he believed in me. He could see my sincere desire to serve God. Like previous pastors, though, he had no idea how to help me. His compassion provided a healing balm for me during that time, however.

---

[2]. Only three people knew of this, a friend I confided in who also struggled with her mental health, my Bible professor, and her son who was the dean. This incident was met with deep compassion by all of them. My Bible professor and her son both assured me of God's love and forgiveness, but because they lacked the knowledge concerning Religious Scrupulosity OCD, they were unable to help me find the peace I so desperately needed. I am forever grateful to them, though, for offering an alternative to the condemnation which otherwise surrounded me. My Bible professor, especially, helped carry me through many dark days.

The suicidal thoughts that had led me to attempt suicide in college continued to plague me, but I fought them as best I could. Reading back through my journal from that time, it is apparent that despair was nearly drowning me. One day, after months of not reading my Bible or praying because of the constant barrage of invasive thoughts, for some now long-forgotten reason, I picked up my Bible, let it fall open, and began to read:

"Blessed be God, even the Father of our Lord Jesus Christ, the Father of mercies, and the God of all comfort; Who comforteth us in all our tribulation, that we may be able to comfort them which are in any trouble, by the comfort wherewith we ourselves are comforted of God. For as the sufferings of Christ abound in us, so our consolation also aboundeth by Christ. And whether we be afflicted, it is for your consolation and salvation, which is effectual in the enduring of the same sufferings which we also suffer: or whether we be comforted, it is for your consolation and salvation. And our hope of you is steadfast, knowing, that as ye are partakers of the sufferings, so shall ye be also of the consolation. For we would not, brethren, have you ignorant of our trouble which came to us in Asia, that we were pressed out of measure, above strength, insomuch that we despaired even of life: But we had the sentence of death in ourselves, that we should not trust in ourselves, but in God which raiseth the dead: Who delivered us from so great a death, and doth deliver: in whom we trust that he will yet deliver us;" (2 Corinthians 1: 3-10 KJV).

A light was turned on in the middle of my darkness as I read. At that moment, I knew God had not abandoned me, and I had hope for the first time in many, many years. God gave me a reason to go on living, that someday God would use what I was going through to help someone else. As I read how Paul had felt "the sentence of death" and had "despaired even of life," I was comforted by the thought that even the great Apostle Paul had gone through deep despair—granted, of a different kind, but despair nonetheless. Paul going on to say that he had trust that someday God would deliver him, spoke a deep hope into my soul that someday God would also deliver me.

This moment in time had a profound impact on me going forward. Although depression and Scrupulosity were still very present, there was a light I now carried inside of me, that like in *The Lord of the Rings* Frodo carried the light of the brightest star, Eärendil, I could bring out that light in the deepest darkness.

I want to be sure I address here that I did not and do not believe God's will was for me to experience what I did in my life. God did not want a little girl to be spiritually and emotionally abused. God did not ordain that I spend my life searching for but never feeling like I could find God, and God certainly did not give me Religious Scrupulosity OCD! I do not believe any of those were part of God's plan for my life. In later chapters, I will address more fully what I have come to know about how God was working throughout my entire life on my behalf. And it is indeed amazing! The promise of Romans 8:28, "And we know that in all things God works for the good of those who love him, who have been called according to his purpose," is not that God will not let anything bad happen to us, but that God can take the ugliest, most horrific things in our lives which were not part of God's plan, and bring beauty from them.

Throughout the rest of my years at college, the preaching and emphasis on "finding your Isaac" to sacrifice to God and the absence of God's felt presence continued to feed my despair. The constant barrage of guilt and shame piled on us by evangelists and preachers in our chapel services was like a continual assault from which we could not escape. We would have spontaneous revivals which would go on for weeks, with the evangelists expressing that they felt there were people holding out on God and they wanted to keep the revival going until those people surrendered. Of course, with the insistent voice of Scrupulosity in my ear, I knew they were talking about me. I would beg God to show me what I was missing in my consecration to God. I would confess stuff I had not done and attitudes I had not had just in case Satan was trying to keep me from remembering I had done them. At one point in my senior year, my boyfriend—whom I fully expected to marry—broke up with me because I could not tell him when I was going to get sanctified, adding to my shame and frustration. How could a person who wanted so desperately to serve God and who loved God so much not figure out how to "find God?"

During my time in college, the pastor at my church, while preaching the same things, extended kindness and compassion to me, though, never condemning me but believing in me. He and his wife treated me like one of their daughters, extending love to me in ways I had scarcely experienced in my life from religious leaders. Thanks in part to them, despite the severity of the depression and Scrupulosity, I survived college.

After graduating, while visiting my parents back in Idaho, I ran into my childhood sweetheart, Norman Peck. We had grown up together in the Nazarene church but had not seen each other in seven years, not since I had left home to live with my relatives in Washington. After a short time of dating (12 days—another story for another time), we eloped, and I moved to Utah, where he was serving in the Air Force.

About two weeks after we were married, after years of trying to hold myself together, I finally suffered a mental breakdown. A combination of factors converged to bring me to that point. While Scrupulosity OCD certainly played its part, it was my lifelong fear of being alone that ultimately caused me to break. Many of the fears throughout my life had been related to the fear of dying, a result of Scrupulosity, I believe. In addition, part of my fear of being alone was fear that I would be emboldened to commit sin. When my new husband went to work, and I was left alone in our house, fear completely paralyzed me. Although I did not have a name for it at the time, my lifetime of fears had led to full-blown Agoraphobia. By definition, Agoraphobia is "a type of anxiety disorder in which you fear and avoid places or situations that might cause you to panic and make you feel trapped, helpless or embarrassed."[3]

Almost overnight, I became nearly incapacitated, unable to leave my house unless accompanied by my husband, and at one point, unable even to leave my living room to go to the restroom unless Norm was at home. (Thankfully, my patient husband was able to come home for lunch each day!) I could not make the simplest choices, like which can of green beans to buy or which pair of socks to wear. Many times in the grocery store, I would have severe panic attacks even though Norm was there with me. The vast number of choices to be made would cause me to shut down completely. I lived in complete fear of dying. I could not plug things into outlets, was scared to ride in a car for fear of an accident, and could not step outside my door for fear that someone would kill me. My obsessive thinking,

---

[3]. https://www.mayoclinic.org/diseases-conditions/agoraphobia/symptoms-causes/syc-20355987

the resulting anxiety, and the compulsions to relieve them took over my entire existence. I could no longer function with the constant barrage of anxiety from the Scrupulosity. Depression was, of course, a major contributing factor. My only thought was, "If I cannot find God, then I do not want to live."

Another significant factor that had been developing for several years but came into full bloom at this time was severe social anxiety. While social anxiety can go hand in hand with Agoraphobia (one fear is of embarrassing oneself in public), my social anxiety was also related to Scrupulosity OCD. Being in public was exhausting for me because I had to thoroughly review in my mind afterward every word I had said, every expression and thought I had during those social interactions to make sure I had not sinned in any way and needed to ask forgiveness. Each social situation was followed by hours of ruminating, which then would result in having to return to the person or persons I was with and apologize—usually for some minor or perceived transgression.

My descent down into the darkness of depression and mental illness was complete. Often, I would sit on the floor in my hallway and feel like the darkness was almost a physical presence that I could see inviting me to give myself completely over to it. My husband would be there with me, telling me he needed me and wanted me to stay with him. During this time, I was not suicidal; I did not want to die. I just did not know how to live with the darkness and emptiness of not being able to know God's presence.

Chapter 3

The Difficulty of Seeking and Receiving Help

"Sometime later, Jesus went up to Jerusalem for one of the Jewish festivals. Now there is in Jerusalem near the Sheep Gate a pool, which in Aramaic is called Bethesda and which is surrounded by five covered colonnades. Here a great number of disabled people used to lie—the blind, the lame, the paralyzed. One who was there had been an invalid for thirty-eight years. When Jesus saw him lying there and learned that he had been in this condition for a long time, he asked him, "Do you want to get well?" (John 5:1-6 NIV)

"Do you want to get well?"

It would be tempting to think Jesus was asking a rhetorical question here. What sick person would not want to get well? Yet, I have come to recognize that just like all the questions Jesus asked, this question penetrated to the heart of the issue. It was…and is…a question of profound importance.

Have you ever considered the impact Jesus' miracles had on those he healed? Think of the man who was born blind. When

Jesus healed him, did Jesus also give the man's brain the ability to interpret what he was seeing, or after having been given the gift of sight, did he have to learn to identify what he was seeing? How did the person born deaf who was healed by Jesus deal with the cacophony of different noises surrounding him? We do not know, of course, if Jesus miraculously gave him the ability to identify what he was hearing, but I tend to think he didn't, and the man had to learn to identify sounds. I like to believe that both the blind man and the deaf man had to learn to live into the healing they had received.

In the darkness of those months following my mental breakdown, healing seemed as impossible to me as it must have to the invalid before Jesus healed him. My days consisted of sitting on the couch, sometimes reading, often sleeping, often dreaming I was suffocating, waking myself gasping for breath. Whenever I did manage to leave the sofa, it was almost like an out-of-body experience; I would look back at the couch to see if my spirit had left my body sitting there. Having never developed a healthy personal identity and having for so long based all my identity in those around me, being alone left me feeling completely devoid of personhood. I could not bear any sounds in the house when Norm was at work, so there was no music, no vacuuming, or even running water to do the dishes. I was incapable of choosing what to make for meals or cooking, so after getting home from a full day of work, Norm would cook and do the cleaning. He never once complained or made me feel bad. He patiently and lovingly cared for me.

Norm had been attending the Nazarene church close to the Air Force Base where we were stationed, so although I still followed all the rules of the conservative holiness church, I attended the Nazarene church with him. Our church family was not aware of what we were going through because as long as I was with Norm, I could function pretty normally. He became the anchor of my identity. I could count on Norm to make all the decisions, and the battles I fought in my mind were invisible to those around me. I was deeply ashamed that I could not feel God's presence or know for sure I was saved, but the people around me saw me as a conscientious Christian who was trying to obey what she thought God wanted. I am guessing that the depression was somewhat apparent, and there were a couple of women in whom I did confide some of my fears and who became dear, supportive friends.

Attending a Church of the Nazarene after being part of the conservative holiness church was disconcerting. The other church had taught so strongly that Nazarenes had backslidden and were living in rebellion against God that I first looked at them through that lens. However, it was not long before I began to experience the love of Jesus through them and knew them to be godly people who loved Jesus and were living for Him. The love they extended to the broken person I was still fills me with warmth.

A little over a year after Norm and I married, our son Brenton was born. It still amazes—and amuses—me that the presence of that tiny, helpless baby was enough to relieve the fear of being alone in my own house. It is not like he could protect me if a big, nasty monster broke in! Now I recognize that, just like all through my life, I had another person to provide me with an identity. For the first time in over a year, I could move freely from one room to another in my house. I still could not go outside my home without Norm, but at least I gained a little bit of freedom.

Having a new baby solved some issues but brought a whole other set of problems with it. One of the most painful aspects of Religious Scrupulosity OCD manifested itself in thoughts of harming my son. After bringing him home from the hospital, the first time I changed his diaper, I had thoughts of molesting him go through my mind. I was filled with the most profound shame imaginable! Quoting Scripture and desperately praying through the tears, I was able to finish changing him but then immediately had Norm take me in to see Brenton's pediatrician. I knew I did not want to hurt my baby, but I was terrified that I must be an evil person because I had that thought go through my head. I brokenly confessed to my son's pediatrician that I was terrified I would molest my son. Being a wise and compassionate man whose area of expertise was trauma to children, he promptly told me that the very fact I had come to him with my concerns made him very sure I would not harm my son. He was right, of course. It was the Scrupulosity making me fearful of sinning. I am deeply grateful to him for his wisdom and compassion.

Nearly two years later, our second child, a daughter, joined our family. Agoraphobia and Scrupulosity still had a firm hold on my life, but for the sake of my children, I did my best to function as well as I could. The depression—although I did not identify it as such yet—still had me living down inside a dark tunnel. Finally, a couple of months after Heidi was born, Norm, who had accompanied me to a medical appointment (for yet another stomachache/headache/etc.), asked my doctor if I could be suffering from depression. My doctor had just published a book on depression, and he pulled it out and began to ask me a series of questions. Sure enough, I had severe depression. Despite having suffered since childhood, I was finally diagnosed with a mental illness for the first time in my life and began to receive help for it. My doctor put me on an antidepressant, but recognizing I also had underlying psychological issues which could not be fixed with medication alone, he recommended I see a counselor.

Seeking counseling was a terrifying thought for me. In the conservative holiness church, counseling was practically forbidden. We were told that counseling was dangerous because it would cause us to excuse sin and foster unforgiveness. With this in mind, I knew if I saw a counselor, it would have to be a Christian and someone from a Wesleyan perspective. I could not possibly (so I thought) see a counselor who might not know about sanctification and living a life free from sin! Naturally, we asked our pastor at the Nazarene church to refer us to a Christian counselor. His response? "I don't believe in counseling. If you will just pray and seek God, you'll be fine."—the very same story I had heard my entire life! Even more disheartening, he began to preach against counseling over the next few weeks. Knowing I needed to be in counseling, we finally made the tough decision to leave that church.

Being stationed in Utah with the military meant there was not another Church of the Nazarene we could attend, so we began to attend a Baptist church with some dear friends. I will never forget that first Sunday morning there. Reading through the bulletin, I saw the church offered classes for Alcoholics Anonymous, Narcotics Anonymous, Codependency, and perhaps one or two others directed at those who struggle with mental health issues and addiction. I was stunned! For the first time in my life, I encountered a church that acknowledged the brokenness people were dealing with in their lives. They did not join in the condemnation and hand-wringing over the world's sinfulness; instead, they attempted to meet people where they were but did it with Christ as the foundation. In that environment, I did not feel like I needed to hide what I was dealing with. Imagine a church that took it as its mission to live out Jesus' admonition that it is not the healthy who need a doctor but the sick!

"Do you want to get well?" Jesus asked.

My first of many choices to say yes to Jesus' question took place just a few weeks after changing churches. While I was praying one day, God began to strip back the layers of hurt, betrayal, and confusion surrounding my heart. God stripped back the church, stripped back my relatives who had dictated God to me, stripped back the depression and fear, and stripped back the outward standards I had clung to as my identity. I felt as if I was standing naked before God. I told God I did not know what to believe anymore, that I did not know what God required from me, and that I wanted to start over as if I had just given my heart to Jesus. I told God I would obey what God told me to do. I knew I could trust the leading of the Holy Spirit to show me what was right and wrong.

Many of us who struggle with chronic illness—be it physical or mental—have found our identity in our illness. It is familiar to us. Saying "Yes!" to Jesus' healing requires us to let go of that identity, that idol, and allow Christ to form a new identity built on who we are in Him. Although the spiritual abuse from the church and my relatives' spiritual and emotional abuse had been painful, the mentally ill person I had become was the only way I knew how to be. Letting go of that and allowing Jesus to start creating a new identity in me is one of the bravest choices I have ever had to make. And, just like the blind man had to learn to identify what he saw and the deaf man had to learn what sounds he was hearing, my healing was one part instantaneous and nine parts hard, hard work.

Very slowly, I began to test the rules of the conservative church to see what I felt God wanted me to do. This was difficult because I had heard preaching that, "If you question (the church's standards), you are already rebelling in your heart, and God will let you believe a lie and go to hell." As I began to wear pants, cut my hair, and wear a wedding ring, as soon as I would start to fear that I was sinning, ==I would sense God's voice asking, "Are you going to obey me, or are you going to obey the (conservative holiness) church?== Are you going to obey me, or will you obey your relatives?" Each time, I answered that I would obey God. It is difficult to convey what a challenge this was with the Scrupulosity OCD always screaming in the background. I was terrified I would be deceived and go to hell! My relatives, of course, thought I was rebelling against God because I did not want to live a holy life. While I did not know then that I had Scrupulosity, I knew they were completely wrong on that point. My whole life had been one long attempt to live a life of "sinless perfection." Specific rules and guidelines are what a person with Scrupulosity longs for!

Two months after that prayer and subsequent personal changes to dress and hair, I had a serious challenge to my choices. My six-month-old daughter, Heidi, was diagnosed with a rare kidney and liver disease, was hospitalized with congestive heart failure, and was not given much hope for survival. I knew my relatives would believe that God was "trying to get hold of me" and that they would believe Heidi's sickness was a direct result of my "rebellion." At the hospital, unable to leave Heidi's room because of the Agoraphobia, all I could do was sit there with her and pray. An amazing step of healing happened there in that room. As I prayed, I recognized that despite being told my whole life that I did not have faith in God, I actually had a tremendous amount of faith! I *knew* God could heal Heidi completely. There was no doubt in my mind. However, I also had faith that God could take care of *me* if Heidi died. Faith was not my problem, after all! In the darkness of the possibility of losing our baby, God began the healing process in me by showing me that I did not lack faith. (Incidentally, Heidi did survive and continues to thrive in her life!)

After adding our third child, Melissa, to our family, I finally started counseling. Because the Agoraphobia was so severe, much of our time was spent working on getting me functioning better in my daily life. Heidi's health was too precarious for us to leave her with a regular babysitter, so when a local nursing agency heard about us, they provided a nurse to care for all of our children for a few hours each week, free of charge. I began to work on leaving the house by myself. There were many times I only made it as far as my driveway or a few blocks down the street, sitting in my car working through the panic attacks. "Do you want to get well? Jesus had asked. "Healing" meant doing the hard work of facing my fears and learning to live life regardless of what was happening inside my mind. Thankfully the medication for the depression relieved some of the darkness and allowed me to work on the Agoraphobia.

From a spiritual perspective, my struggle with doubting my salvation and being unable to experience God's felt presence continued to plague me. Like many with Scrupulosity, I had learned to compartmentalize a bit by avoiding things that triggered the Scrupulosity. For many years, I would go back and forth between being unable to read my Bible and attempting to read it daily, being unable to pray and then trying to pray faithfully, thinking about God, and then being unable to think about God. Sometimes I would go a couple of months doing fairly well mentally, but then I would realize I hadn't thought about God in a while, and my sorrow over my perceived lack of relationship with God would kick back in. I would focus on drawing near to God again, only to have the Scrupulosity come back full force. For a person who from childhood had never wanted anything but to love and serve God faithfully, this was exceedingly painful and would plunge me again and again into despair.

Through all of this, though, the Religious Scrupulosity OCD was never identified. My counselors and I did identify and talk about spiritual abuse as having triggered depression and agoraphobia. Still, our focus was primarily on issues of low self-image, phobias, and discussing that God is a loving God (something I did not doubt, by the way!) Having also been diagnosed with Generalized Anxiety Disorder, we worked on how to manage that as well. Neither my Christian counselors nor my non-Christian counselors recognized that the leading cause of the depression, anxiety, and phobias was instead Religious Scrupulosity OCD. Part of this, I am sure, is that I did not talk with them about my "spiritual issues." Those things I took to my pastors or tried to deal with by myself.

Because confession to a religious authority can be a powerful compulsion with Scrupulosity, each of my pastors was dutifully informed that I did not know if I was saved, let alone sanctified. In fact, I had stopped using any such terms to describe my relationship with God because they triggered such intense doubts, and I was afraid of lying. I would tell my pastors that while I did not know my spiritual status, I was nevertheless trying to live a life of obedience to God. My pastors heard about my fear of committing the unpardonable sin; they heard confessions about my fear of blaspheming God. They heard about the deep shame I felt over some of my inner thoughts. It is sometimes tempting to be ashamed or embarrassed about the things I told my pastors because some were of such a personal nature. I have learned to be kind to myself, though, realizing that I was driven to confess by the Scrupulosity.

Because my husband was in the military for twenty-seven years, we moved around a lot, and with each new move, we had a new church with a new pastor to whom I had to go with my "spiritual problems." I am blessed to have had incredible pastors over the years. Each one of them did their best to help and encourage me. It was often through assuring me that they knew I was a Christian; they just thought I was overly conscientious. I will talk more in a later chapter about how pastors and religious leaders can help those with Scrupulosity.

Despite my best efforts, there were significant ways my having Scrupulosity impacted my husband and children. As mentioned, I relied on Norm for nearly everything, insisting he accompany me anytime I left the house, expecting him to make any phone calls that needed to be made, and running interference in social situations. My children had to deal with rules which made little sense to them but that I insisted were necessary as Christians. They dealt with the frustration of my being unable to make decisions and the angry outbursts when the anxiety would escalate to the point of being unbearable. Although I bear many regrets about those things, I have had to learn to extend grace to myself, knowing I was doing the best I could to survive something I did not understand and did not know how to deal with.

From the time I was first diagnosed with depression, anxiety, and agoraphobia, I talked openly about it with everyone in my life. Even in the earliest days of being on medication and counseling, I was determined not to perpetuate the stigma of mental illness I had grown up with. Each place we lived, I had friends who offered encouragement and support, and without whom I would not have been able to make the progress that I did.

My pastors and other religious leaders—other than the one I described earlier—were completely supportive of my being on medication and being in counseling. After a medication I was on caused me to be psychotic, one pastor not only talked with me during my brain having gone haywire, but he convinced me to go to the hospital, personally took me, and daily visited me. My pastors never shamed me or blamed me. I could tell, though, that my situation was frustrating to them, and they did not know how to help me. My own neediness was deeply embarrassing to me, and at times I could tell my presence proved to be challenging to my pastors. Despite that, they patiently walked through my darkness with me, encouraging me all the while. It is impossible to overstate how important that was to my healing process.

It is difficult for me to write, then, as I will in a later chapter, about how my pastors, other religious leaders, family, and friends unintentionally made my healing more of a challenge. It feels disloyal. However, I am convinced that every one of them would have appreciated and taken advantage of having information that would have helped them minister better to me.

This is why I am writing this book. This is why I am passionate about educating pastors and other religious leaders about Scrupulosity. Although I had suffered from Scrupulosity for most of my life, it was not until eight years ago that I was finally diagnosed with it! It was not a counselor or a pastor who recognized it, but a woman I had never met in person and whose name I do not even remember. She was part of an online Nazarene fellowship group I was part of for many years. About nine years ago, I started sharing a little more openly in that group some of the "spiritual issues" I was having. Some of the responses were supportive, but several people gave me the same old answers of needing to have more faith. "If you're feeling far from God," they said, "you're the one who moved." However, one woman in that group contacted me privately to tell me I sounded just like her husband, who has something called "Religious Scrupulosity Obsessive Compulsive Disorder." I immediately went online and did research, and for the first time in my life, I had a name for what I had been struggling with for so long. It was like reading my own life story! While I was thrilled to have answers finally, it was equally distressing that throughout nearly forty years of suffering, twenty-five years (off and on) of counseling, and a lifetime of being in church, not one person recognized I had Religious Scrupulosity OCD.

My counselors are perhaps at fault for not recognizing and diagnosing my Scrupulosity. However, it would not have been readily apparent because I did not talk to them about the spiritual issues I struggled with. After being diagnosed, I contacted a couple of my previous (Christian) counselors who, surprisingly, had not even been aware of a type of obsessive-compulsive disorder called Religious Scrupulosity. In addition, I reached out to several of my previous pastors, none of whom had ever heard of it. I cannot help but feel that if just one of my pastors, Sunday school teachers, or mentors over the years had been knowledgeable about Scrupulosity, I could perhaps have avoided years…decades…of suffering.

I do need to note that although the Religious Scrupulosity OCD was not diagnosed until I was in my late forties, I had still made significant progress in my healing journey over the years. Counseling and medication helped me deal with the depression. Learning important life skills enabled me to function better in my life. Other types of obsessions and compulsions which were identified (such as checking and re-checking door locks, and germ obsessions) were treated with the same skills I would later need to deal with the Scrupulosity OCD. Spiritually, God had faithfully worked in my life, loving me, growing me, and healing me when I was not even aware of God's presence. All along the way, at every step, I had to answer yes to Jesus' question, "Do you want to get well?" It was hard work sometimes, but choosing to take medication, getting counseling, working on functioning better in my life, and purposely pursuing a relationship with God despite the challenges were all part of me saying "Yes!" to Jesus. Having done so much work on so many aspects of my life—mental, emotional, spiritual, and social—I was already well on my way with the tools I would need to deal with the Scrupulosity once it was identified.

It is important for my readers to know that my journey back toward healing has not been a straight line, nor always climbing upwards. It has been more like a meandering path with lots of ups and downs, many times of darkness followed by moments of light. I am an advocate for taking the appropriate medications which can help with mental illness, but my own experience with them was not always easy. Twice my antidepressants made me psychotic, once requiring hospitalization. Another time (while I was in the hospital for psychosis) I had a serious allergic reaction to an antidepressant. Still another one caused permanent hearing loss and tinnitus, resulting in my psychiatrist taking me off all antidepressants.

I say all that to make the point that medications are not a magic cure, but they can help the process. When one does not work, we consult with our doctor and try something else. Counseling does not "fix" you, either. Healing is grueling work sometimes! Trauma does long-term damage to the ways our brains and bodies work, and getting a diagnosis, taking a pill, or being anointed for healing does not instantaneously fix what the trauma broke in us. For me, the process continues to this day. Even as I am writing this book, I am learning and growing, putting together pieces in my own puzzle which were missing or misplaced.

Before moving on to explore how a person deals with Scrupulosity and how to minister to those with it, though, there are a couple of aspects about it that need further explanation. In the following couple of chapters, I will describe some particular challenges faced by those with Scrupulosity, especially as they relate to experiences within the church.

Part II

Three Challenges Inherent to Scrupulosity

Chapter 4

Challenge #1: Drowning In Shame

'*I can't weep!*' *Francis' voice was sharp with pain.* '*How must I weep? I couldn't bear to weep. There is no one ... it hurts too much ... I could never stop ... I can't weep.*' *His hand moved in a gesture of hopelessness, and he got up from the hearth and knelt before the abbot.*

'Father, I confess my fault. I ask God's forgiveness and yours.' The words were torn wretchedly from the centre of him, little shreds of his soul ripped away in pleading need. He was trembling, his head bent, his hands clasped together.

[Father Peregrine]: 'My son, what is it you want me to forgive? Are you asking me to forgive the pain of your heart? God knows—'

'Me,' Francis broke out in anguish. 'I need you to forgive me. I want to be clean. I want to be true... I want to belong to God... I want him to forgive me.'

'I don't want him to leave me alone.' Peregrine heard the note of shame, of reluctance, and understood that this was the heart of the thing.

> `I am so terrified he will abandon me. I don't deserve him, I'm not good enough, I'm not clean or pure or holy. I dread his coldness, his turning away ... Oh, I'm so afraid of burning in hell. I would do anything, I ... I am a desert place, useless and poor. Oh God, forgive me ... forgive me ... not only my sins, but me. Oh, do not leave me alone, don't abandon me....* [4]

In one of the most heart-wrenching and beautiful stories in her entire incredible series, *The Hawk and the Dove*, Penelope Wilcock captures the heart of what many of us—not just those with Scrupulosity—deal with. It is shame. I do not know who first pointed out that the difference between guilt and shame is that guilt says "I did something bad," while shame says "I am bad," but it succinctly captures that reality.

Over the years, I have read many books about different kinds of abuse and how abuse affects a person's relationship with God. Many people cannot easily call God "Father" because of how their earthly father treated them. Still others are afraid of God and feel like God is waiting for them to make a mistake so God can send them to hell. Suffering abuse or trauma often causes people to be angry at God, and many more quit believing in God altogether.

Those reactions are, of course, true for many people. Our view of God is shaped by our interactions with our parents, our churches, and those in positions of religious authority over us, such as pastors and Sunday school teachers. Often, people who have experienced spiritual abuse view God as just waiting

---

4. Penelope Wilcock. The Hawk and the Dove Trilogy (3-in-1 Volume) (Kindle Locations 2729-2739). Kindle Edition. (Used with Permission.)

to send them to hell for the slightest sin. Many see God as unloving.

While this is the experience of many people, it is not true for all of us. A truth that I know some of us experience is that we do not see God that way. Despite the abuse we have suffered and the difficulties we have faced, our view of God has remained positive. We still see God as loving, just, and merciful. For us, God is not the problem. Instead—and to a degree perhaps, rightly so—we see ourselves as the problem. I am not talking here about understanding that we are sinners in need of a savior. Instead, I am referring to a deep self-loathing some of us experience as a result, specifically, of abuse or of an incorrect understanding of how God views us.

From my earliest childhood, the church I attended did a good job of making sure I knew I was a sinner. My relatives joined in the chorus, constantly reminding me I was a sinner on my way to hell. The emotional abuse went beyond that, however. There was an underlying current of contempt my siblings and I, as well as our mother, endured from relatives and from members of the church. It was not tied directly to our actions or anything we could pinpoint as the reason why they would feel that way toward us. Without knowing what I had done or was doing to—as I thought—invite their contempt, I instead came to believe I was somehow worthy of that contempt. I deserved it because I was a sinner. I learned to internalize contempt for myself at the deepest levels.

I have discovered this is the case for many of us who struggle with Scrupulosity OCD. We see ourselves as so sinful that we come to loathe ourselves. When a church emphasizes sin without balancing it with the good news of the gospel, it damages people. It was not that we were not taught how to "be saved," but that we were taught it from the perspective of being saved to avoid hell. It was not about God loving us or about how our eternal life with Christ could start in the here and now, it was only about making sure our hearts were right with God because we could die any minute and go to hell.

Is it any wonder, then, that Scrupulosity became such an integral part of my whole personality and how self-loathing gained such a hold over me? Yet, what most people who talk about abuse emphasize is how much people hate God or fear God without realizing that there is a whole other dynamic at play in many people's lives—intense self-loathing.

For a person with Scrupulosity OCD, this can be a dangerous underlying problem. For me, it led to a ritualistic "beating my body into submission." Whipping myself to show God how sorry I was for my sin was part of why I did it, but the other part was a way to take out my anger on myself for my failure to live a holy life. I deserved punishment, and I was going to make sure I got it.

Self-loathing based on seeing oneself as extremely sinful is a dangerous aspect of Scrupulosity OCD. Our constant failure to live perfect lives—free from all sin in thought, word, and deed—provides constant fodder for self-loathing. For a person with Scrupulosity, there is no separation between what I think and who I am. Scriptures taken completely out of context, like, "As a man thinketh in his heart, so is he…" (Proverbs 23:7 KJV) have been used by religious people in such a way that we heap guilt on ourselves for every stray thought. (In fact, I did not know until five minutes ago when I looked up Proverbs 23 and read the verse in its context in several different versions, that I realized it has nothing to do with how we think but was instead used in a very specific context!) So, with Scrupulosity we think: if I have a thought about molesting my son, then I must be a child molester. If a thought crosses my mind that I could steal a necklace from the store, I am a thief. If I think about eating a piece of chocolate even though I have vowed to give it up, I must be weak and unfaithful, even idolatrous. If I see an attractive person and the thought crosses my mind that I would like to spend time with them, then I must be an adulterer. The constant barrage of disappointment and hatred we internalize can have devastating consequences on our perceptions of ourselves.

The self-loathing I heaped on myself was a horrible burden to bear! Often, looking in the mirror was nearly impossible because I couldn't look myself in the eye due to the deep shame I felt over the labels I had plastered all over myself. God was justified in turning God's back on me, I thought, because I was a despicable person! I constantly called myself horrible names and beat myself up mentally and physically for being so evil.

Perhaps nothing so completely encapsulates how I viewed myself as two images I carried inside for many years. Most of us are familiar with what psychologists call our "inner child," that part of ourselves that carries our childhood memories and experiences. Sometimes people experience this inner child as just a smaller version of themselves, a cute innocent child who is playful and joyful. But, for people who have suffered abuse, our inner child can seem small and vulnerable. Many counselors approach helping people heal by helping them first learn to meet the needs of the inner child which went unmet in childhood. Far from being "pop psychology," this method has tried-and-true results.

The first time a counselor mentioned "inner child" to me, I was flabbergasted! I knew exactly who he was talking about, but I did not know it was a real thing. I had never talked about the little girl inside of me for fear people would think I was crazy or had "multiple personalities." I knew that was not the case, but I did not know what else to call it. I was relieved, then, to know this was normal.

For me, the little girl inside was young, maybe six or seven. She had the saddest eyes. In my mental picture of her, she was filthy dirty, with grimy hair and a tear-streaked face. Worst of all, I had mentally put her in a metal cage in the "basement" of my deepest inner self, where whenever I thought she was misbehaving, I would go down and slap and kick her—slap and kick myself. Oh, I knew that little girl well. She is the one who bore the brunt of my self-loathing. She was full of shame and grief, huddling in the farthest corner she could find.

As an adult, whenever someone would mention how we view ourselves, I would immediately see the other image with which I identified myself. If you have seen the movie "The Little Mermaid," you may remember the "poor unfortunate souls" enslaved by Ursula. They are ugly, twisted creatures held captive by Ursula, with hopeless eyes and ghastly, pleading expressions. That was the image I saw of myself. I was despicable and deserved to be miserable because I was so sinful. God was right in turning God's back on me, I thought.

By completely internalizing the blame, I could still view God as totally loving, just, and holy. Throughout the decades of internal torture, I loved God and deeply desired to serve God and allow Jesus to make me more like Himself. I desperately wanted to have a relationship with God. I loved going to church and loved our church family wherever we were. Any negative comments I received had to be because I deserved them for being so sinful and dirty. Any healing that would come for my mental illness, then, had to start with recognizing and dealing with the self-loathing.

This is no doubt true, also, for many who do not have Scrupulosity. Over the years, I cannot tell you how many people have told me they were surprised I still went to church and still loved God. I am convinced this is because a lot of people blame God and the church for their suffering. But for those of us who internalize it instead and turn it into self-loathing, God and the church remain an important part of our lives. I would suggest that if there is a person who has suffered significant abuse but who does not blame God or the church, then that person could perhaps be struggling instead with self-loathing. This goes far beyond the low self-esteem we often see and talk about. Low self-esteem is a state of being, while self-loathing is an active, aggressive pummeling of self. As we interact with others, I think it is worth being aware of this distinction.

My journey toward healing from self-loathing began several years before I was diagnosed with Religious Scrupulosity OCD. Of course, much of my counseling over the years tried to deal with "low self-esteem" and help "heal the inner child," but not recognizing the source and severity of the self-loathing made it difficult to make progress. Despite that, God was working in me to bring healing.

One summer about fifteen years ago, I got up the courage to go to a Ladies' Retreat with the women from my church. While my social anxiety was still significant, making it difficult for me to go places—especially without Norm—at this particular church, I had a couple of friends with whom I had shared my difficulties who said they would be there to help me throughout the retreat. Another part of my angst about going was my fear that while everyone else was experiencing

God's presence more deeply, I would be left out. That usually led to a deepening of depression. However, I also loved God and wanted to draw near to Him. I thought maybe *this time* I might finally be able to "find" God.

Our focus for the retreat was Psalm 139, a text I had always struggled with. Not only did it not seem true that God was with me everywhere, but verse fourteen had always been a difficult one for me: "I will praise you because I am fearfully and wonderfully made. Your works are wonderful, I know that full well." That just did not seem true for me; I was not fearfully and wonderfully made—I was sinful and dirty. Having to share about my relationship (or lack thereof) with other ladies around the table was humiliating and depressing because I did not feel like I had a relationship with God.

Again, I need to stress that I did not think God was the problem—I thought I was the problem. I had been taught that God cannot dwell where there is sin, so because I could not seem to experience His presence, I must be sinful. Being at a retreat where women were experiencing the rich presence of God while I was seemingly cut off from God was crushing to my heart.

Our retreat was held at Trinity Pines Camp and Conference Center in Cascade, Idaho, a beautiful facility surrounded by forest, with views of the mountains and a lake nearby. The retreat was indeed difficult in some of the ways I had feared. In addition, being in an extended social situation also took its toll on me; having to constantly guard myself to be sure I was not lying, not exaggerating, not hurting anyone's feelings, etc., was completely exhausting.

One of the activities the women at the retreat decided to do was a zipline. At the time, at 600 feet, it was the longest zipline in the state of Idaho. The fear of heights was perhaps my worst fear of all the many fears I had. From childhood I had been terrified of heights, completely freezing and being unable to move, and being filled with panic. Even climbing a ladder could trigger that fear. It was so bad that even as a child, I could not walk across a bridge without intense panic. (A huge part of the fear was driven by Scrupulosity, though, because I did not fear falling as much as I feared I would lose my mind for a moment and jump to my death.) Doing a zipline, then, seemed like a very bad idea. Social anxiety was a close second to my fear of heights, though. It insisted I must not do anything to draw attention to myself or seem "less-than" those around me, so when invited to do the zipline, I agreed. I did not want to look like a coward

I started at the end of the line, and the closer I got to the front, the greater my fear began to grow. The argument inside my head was intense, and I almost backed out of doing the zipline, but at the last minute, I told myself that I would lose respect for myself and regret it for the rest of my life if I did not do it. I signed my life away on the form that said I would not hold them liable if something bad happened, and I let them hook me into the harness. To get to the zipline, we had to climb up steps nailed into a tree. That part was not too bad, but stepping onto the postage-stamp-sized platform was terrifying. At least climbing up I had the tree to hold onto and block my view of how high I was! I hugged the tree as the man on the platform hooked my harness to the zipline.

As I turned away from the tree and faced the nothingness in front of me, I was completely paralyzed with fear. I started crying hysterically from the intensity of the panic attack I was having. I could not physically move I was so overcome with fear. The rule of the zipline is that you must step off of the platform yourself; the worker will not push you. You have two choices: leave the platform by way of the zipline or climb back down the tree. I did not think I could do either!

I do not know how long I was trapped there, but it seemed like a very long time. The man there on the platform with me offered gentle words of encouragement and compassion, never once berating me. He told me I could sit down and slide off the platform if I needed to, as opposed to stepping off, so I sat down. Finally, I said, "Okay, God, here we go!" and I scooted off the platform.

The initial drop to let my weight be transferred to the zipline was terrifying, then I was on my way! Bawling my eyes out and completely terrified, I zipped along. About halfway across, though, my stubbornness kicked in and I struck a lovely Superman pose for just a few seconds. Then I was barreling towards the end of the zipline where people waited to catch me safely. Incredibly, I had faced my greatest fear and I had survived!

As my friends met me on the other side and we walked back to the cabin, I could not stop crying. It was like a dam had broken inside of me and there was no holding back. I cried for hours, sometimes sobbing. For a person who "cries once a year just to make sure everything works right," this was disconcerting. It was a healing cry, though, like a pressure-relief valve releasing years of pent-up shame and anger at myself.

Every little while for the rest of that afternoon and evening, I would find tears just flowing down my face. I had no control over it and did not understand why I was so emotional. Even as I lay in bed that night saying my evening prayers, the tears flowed. The next morning before breakfast, I got up and decided to have my devotional time outside. As I sat on a bench looking around at all the beauty, I began to pray and thank God for His beautiful creation. "God, those trees are part of your beautiful creation! Those mountains are part of your beautiful creation. Those flowers are part of your beautiful creation. That lake is part of your beautiful creation." Then in the quiet sacredness of that moment, I heard God whisper to me, "And so are you!"

Never in my life had I considered myself part of God's beautiful creation! Instead, I had seen myself as a result of what went wrong in the Garden of Eden. I was a result of the Fall. Like David in the Psalms, I thought, "Surely I was sinful at birth, sinful from the time my mother conceived me." (Psalm 51:5) God, however, sees me differently! He sees me as part of His beautiful creation! God had begun to help me rewrite my self-narrative, and deep healing was beginning to take place.

From that moment forward, anytime I would start to internally berate myself or call myself unkind names, I was reminded, "Don't talk that way to someone who is part of God's beautiful creation!" This was a huge change! No more calling myself stupid, pitiful, or worse. No more mentally slapping myself when I thought I said something stupid. Instead, I was given the freedom through God's gracious gift of recognizing that even though I was not perfect, God loved me and saw me as beautiful. I was often reminded of God's words to Peter, "Do not call impure anything that God has made clean." (Acts 10:15 NIV) This, too, was a way I said "Yes!" to Jesus' question, "Do you want to get well?"

That was, of course, just the beginning of a very long journey. The internal dialogue I had lived with for so long was not quickly and easily replaced. To this day I must remind myself that my identity is based in who God is and what God has done for me. Countering self-condemning thoughts with truths built on God instead of on myself was important. The words I use, then, are not self-glorifying positive affirmations aimed at building myself up but are instead about God. "I will treat myself as one made in the image of God. I will treat myself as one Jesus loves and died to save." Finding my worth and value in Christ changes how I view and treat myself.

I have often concluded my zipline story by saying that it changed my life forever. Not only is this true because of how God showed me how God sees me, which then affected how I see and treat myself, but also because of how having the courage to face my greatest fear changed how I viewed myself. My life up to that point was focused on doing things with the least risk. I was as opposite of an adrenaline junkie as one could be. I was convinced I was a complete coward but was usually too frightened to act any differently. It took an incredible amount of courage to do the zipline. Doing so loosened the grip of self-loathing, which in turn, I believe opened me up to receiving God's view of me. It also gave me a foundation for facing my many other fears, one by one, and continues to this day to help me refuse to be controlled by fear.

For those who are dealing with self-loathing or other issues related to your identity, perhaps my story can provide you with the hope that you, too, can find healing. It is important, though, not to take my story as "the way" in which God works in a person's life. God's healing will look different in your life or the lives of those you care about than it looks in mine. So many of us look for the right formula, the right prayer, the right self-help book to tell us how we can get God to heal us. The sad reality is that there are those who will claim their way as "the way" but cause more harm as people are left empty and disappointed that God did not work in their lives in the same way. This can, in turn, cause more self-loathing or further anger at God. Instead of this, I would encourage each person to be open to how God is working in their own life, trusting that God will help in ways that are unique to them.

On a similar note, we have explored a bit how religious beliefs and experiences are an avenue through which Scrupulosity attacks an individual. Outside influences, such as religious observances, doctrines, and the Bible or other religious books used in an abusive way, can cause significant harm to people and be triggers for Scrupulosity. I am intrigued by how those very avenues which caused harm, though, can also be avenues of healing. God worked within my religious framework to bring healing. As the reader will realize throughout the rest of this book, God worked in me to correct wrong beliefs and reframed Scriptures that had condemned me into Scriptures which, when rightly understood, brought healing. I did not need to abandon my religious framework in order to find healing. God, true to Jesus' promise, is continuing to "guide me into all truth."

Developing a healthier view of myself based on how God sees me has been an integral part of my healing. Being diagnosed with Scrupulosity a few years later helped tremendously, too. Self-loathing is just one of the major issues individuals with Scrupulosity deal with, however. In the next chapter, we will explore one of the most difficult and destructive aspects of Scrupulosity—unwanted and intrusive thoughts—and how that contributes to self-loathing and the debilitating nature of Scrupulosity.

Chapter 5

Challenge #2: You Are What You Think

"Guilty, as charged."

The words hung suspended in the air before rippling out to fill every corner of the courtroom. Faces filled with dismay and sorrow lined one side of the aisle while on the other side, faces shone with relief tinged with their own brand of sorrow.

"Guilty." With the sharp rap of the judge's gavel, it was over. Shackles encircled wrists, and hands reached out to escort the convicted from the courtroom—another child molester behind bars.

Meanwhile, I sat safely ensconced at home, with no shackles, no escort to lead me away, not guilty in the world's eyes, but arrested, tried, and convicted in my own mind. The thought of molesting my child had crossed my mind, so I thought I was just as guilty. Didn't I deserve prison? In the tortured expanse of my inmost being, I called myself the name "child molester." I deserved punishment.

On another day, I applied the label "thief" to myself as the thought of shoplifting a candy bar crossed my mind. Still another day, I was a "liar" as I thought about not giving all the details of a story. "Murderer," I shouted at myself when a stray thought of smothering my child crossed my mind or when the notion of ending my own life intruded into my thoughts. "Guilty! Guilty! Guilty!" And, oh the shame—shame that stripped away every shred of self-respect and dignity I possessed. There are no words strong enough to describe the shame—and as I mentioned in the previous chapter, self-loathing—which overtook my life as I pronounced myself guilty of the most horrible and despicable sins, all based on stray thoughts which had drifted through my mind.

The psychological phenomenon I was dealing with is known as "Moral Thought-Action Fusion," and is extremely common not just in Religious Scrupulosity OCD, but in many anxiety-based mental disorders. Thought-Action Fusion "refers to the belief that thoughts and actions are inextricably linked."[5] There are two types of Thought-Action Fusion, Moral TAF, and Likelihood TAF. "'Moral' TAF is the belief that unacceptable thoughts are morally equivalent to overt unacceptable actions."[6] In other words, people with Moral Thought-Action Fusion (M-TAF) believe that if they think a thought, they are guilty of the act. No matter how random or removed a thought is from the person's character and desires, if they have a thought about committing a sin, then they feel they are guilty of that sin and in need of confession and forgiveness. This is what I experienced over and over throughout my life with intrusive and unwanted thoughts.

---

5. Thought-action fusion: Review of the literature and future directions. Clinical Psychology Review 25 (2005) 263-284. David Berle and Vladan Starcevic.
6. IBID

Another type of Thought-Action Fusion is known as Likelihood Thought-Action Fusion (L-TAF). L-TAF is a belief that thinking or wishing something bad would happen to someone makes it more likely that it will happen. If, for instance, I think someone will get in a car accident, then the likelihood of that happening increases. A person with L-TAF believes that their thoughts can make bad things happen either to themselves or to others. This type of thinking has been called "magical thinking." In a similar way to those with M-TAF, the person with Scrupulosity who suffers from L-TAF will try to ward off or neutralize their thoughts, sometimes even taking steps to try to prevent a tragedy from happening. While this was less of a problem for me personally, many with Scrupulosity struggle more with this type of Thought-Action Fusion. Both types of Thought-Action Fusion are common with anxiety and obsessive-compulsive type mental disorders.

Much research into Thought-Action Fusion has taken place over the years. The way thoughts are formed in our minds has long intrigued researchers, prompting them to study how and why some people are more prone to TAF than others. While there are several variables, one valuable research found that "the interaction between three variables (i.e., shame-proneness, thought action fusion-morality beliefs and obsessions) predicts compulsions. The relationship between obsessions and compulsions was stronger as a function of shame-proneness and thought action fusion-morality beliefs, such that the highest levels of compulsions were found for those who had the highest levels on all three predictors."[7] For individuals who carry much

---

[7]. Believing that Intrusive Thoughts Can be Immoral Moderates the Relationship Between Obsessions and Compulsions for Shame-prone Individuals. Springer Science+Business Media, LLC 2008, David P. Valentiner, Sarah A Smith.

shame, who see a strong link between their thoughts and being guilty of the action even though it was only in their thoughts, and who are deeply conscientious, compulsions—and thus Religious Scrupulosity OCD—is a predictable outcome.

Can you see the echoes of my own story in this research? Shame and Thought-Action-Fusion, along with religious obsessions about holiness and sinlessness, combined to form full-blown Religious Scrupulosity OCD in me.

Every day, our brains are bombarded with information. Without conscious thought, our brains store away images and experiences, constantly learning and cataloging. Billboards, signs, television and radio programs, stories on social media, newspaper stories, overheard conversations, books we read, meetings we attend—the list could go on and on—provide a never-ending flow to our brains, and we take it in without even realizing it.

This was brought home to me rather recently in an amusing way. A nine-year-old boy on the Autism Spectrum was riding with his mom and sister in their van. His younger sister asked their mom for the name of our current president in America. She responded, "President Biden." The nine-year-old, pleased that he knew some additional information, piped up, "I know his full name! It's Sue Joe Biden!" All over the valley where they live, he had seen a plethora of signs with that message boldly written on them. His brain had stored that totally insignificant (to a nine-year-old) piece of information until something had sparked that memory.

Our brains do this all the time, storing random information and then bringing it back for our consideration when something sparks the memory. For instance, a person may see a news program about a mother drowning her children in the bathtub. The next day as that person is bathing their own child, the thought might cross their mind that they could drown their child. The majority of people recognize those thoughts don't have any moral significance in and of themselves. They are just random thoughts to be met with an, "Oh, that's weird!" or "Creepy!" or a simple shrug of the shoulders dismissing it to the realm of insignificance again. But for a person with Thought-Action Fusion, it is a completely different story. There is no difference to them between thinking a thought and being guilty of the action. If I thought about drowning my child, I am as guilty of murder as if I had indeed done it.

Intrusive or unwanted thoughts are common and not limited to any particular population or mental illness. We all store information and our brains do not discriminate between "good" thoughts and "bad" thoughts on their own. In one sense, our brains are kind of like a stream of water flowing along with all kinds of information. Occasionally, a thought will rise to the surface like a twig in a stream. Most people can let the thought go right on down the stream without inspecting it, but for people with Scrupulosity, we see the twig and think a tree is growing in the middle of the stream. We think we must kill the tree, but in so doing, we disrupt the flow of the stream, causing more and more twigs to appear. While not a perfect illustration, perhaps it helps to understand how a person with Scrupulosity views random unwanted or intrusive thoughts, why they seem to get stuck in the scrupulous mind, and how the compulsions we use to try to dislodge them instead cause them to be a bigger problem.

Thoughts are just part of the process, however. The moral significance we apply to those thoughts is at the heart of what leads to the devastating shame and compulsions to wash away or neutralize the thoughts. For many of us raised in a church environment, we have long heard—and without proper discipling, interpreted—that our thoughts are a result of the condition of our hearts. Scriptures such as Matthew 15:19 seem to say precisely that: "For out of the heart come evil thoughts—murder, adultery, sexual immorality, theft, false testimony, slander." Jesus Himself taught that if a person lusts after someone in their hearts, they are guilty of adultery. What are we to make of Scriptures which say that if we are in Christ, "the new creation has come. The old has gone, the new is here," (2 Corinthians 5:17), and the many, many Scriptures which talk about being cleansed from all sin, and that God will give us a new heart? For a person with Scrupulosity, all those Scriptures point to the "fact" that because we still have evil thoughts going through our minds, we must not really be saved. We must still be evil.

As a young Christian, I was taught that bad thoughts were either from my own sinful heart or, if I was saved, then they were from Satan trying to get me to sin. The ways the church taught me to deal with this were in fact exactly the ways that people with Scrupulosity deal with them! We were told to "plead the blood of Jesus," which I understood to mean praying that because I was a Christian, Jesus' blood would protect me from Satan's attacks. We were also taught to memorize Scripture to ward off bad thoughts. Singing a Christian song was yet another way to neutralize intrusive thoughts, as was praying. Are these good things? Yes! Are they helpful in countering bad thoughts? Yes! *Unless* you have Religious Scrupulosity OCD.

For a person with Scrupulosity, doing the above things to ward off or neutralize bad thoughts makes them occur more often. It is a vicious cycle! The more a person actively tries not to think about the offending thought, the more often it occurs because the person is spending so much time and energy on it. In Chapter 1, I talked about the fact that because compulsions (in this case, praying, quoting Scripture, etc.) relieve the anxiety, it gives credence to the seriousness of the thought. So, for instance, if I have a thought about cheating on a test, the anxiety will start to grow inside of me that I must be a bad person, a thief, and a liar. If I do not do something, I might go to hell. So, I quote John 3:16, or I sing "Jesus Loves Me." Amazingly, I feel better! Well, if I feel better, then that must mean I really was evil to think about cheating. The next time the thought of cheating goes through my mind, I am primed to take it as a serious issue and do the compulsion—praying, singing, quoting Scripture—to deal with it. Each time I do that, I am reinforcing and making the original thought into a larger and larger issue.

Learning how to deal with unwanted and intrusive thoughts is one of the greatest challenges of Scrupulosity and other mental illnesses. For me, one of the most helpful things was understanding how our brains store information and that merely having a thought was not the same as thinking about something. Like the metaphor I used earlier about the stream of thoughts, a twig (stray thought) drifting by has no moral rightness or wrongness. It is simply a piece of information my brain has stored. The point where it perhaps becomes sinful, if you will, is when I pick it up and consider that I might do what it suggests, which then reveals the condition of my heart. Scriptures like Proverbs 23:7 "For as he thinketh in his heart, so is he," (KJV) bear this out. The Hebrew word for "thinketh" carries the meaning of "to calculate" or "to reckon."[8] It is ac-

---

[8] https://biblehub.com/hebrew/8176.htm

tive participation in thinking about something, as opposed to having the thought go through one's mind. (As I mentioned earlier, Proverbs 23:7 is used in a specific context.)

It is important, I think, to affirm the words of the Bible that our thoughts matter. What we choose to think about does indeed reveal the condition of our hearts. However, it is equally important to realize that just because a thought crosses our minds does not mean we have chosen to think about it. For those of us with Scrupulosity, it can be challenging because, in order to lessen the frequency of intrusive thoughts, we must learn not to ward them off, in essence, to learn how to let them flow on down the stream without attaching any moral character to them. In Chapter 7, I will talk more about the tools a person with Scrupulosity or other anxiety disorders can use to lessen the frequency and hold intrusive and unwanted thoughts have on us and how pastors and other religious leaders can be supportive in furthering the understanding of the difference between stray thoughts and thoughts originating from a sinful heart.

There were few things more distressing to me as a deeply conscientious Christian doing my best to be holy and serve God with my whole heart than the blasphemous thoughts which my brain casually tossed up for my brain to consider. Blasphemy, I knew, would condemn me eternally to life without God, a possibility I could not even bear to contemplate. I kept a constant "guard" on my thoughts trying to prevent any blasphemous thoughts from sneaking through. Desperately begging the Holy Spirit to forgive me whenever it happened, was not enough to keep me from living in constant fear. I knew I must be very evil to have thoughts like that, yet I also knew how much I loved God and wanted to have a relationship with God. The two seemed totally incongruent to me, but not knowing how to resolve that, I tried, instead, to avoid any activity which triggered blasphemous thoughts, like reading my Bible or praying.

One topic of those intrusive thoughts, though, was even more horrifying to me and nearly beyond my capacity to handle: sexual thoughts about God. It is tempting to skip over this topic entirely as it deals with some of the most personal and excruciatingly painful aspects of my experience with Scrupulosity. That, I know, is shame trying to talk its way back into my story, but I refuse to be held captive by the false narrative with which shame tries to choke the truth and keep it hidden in some dark corner. If I do not talk about it, I heap shame back on myself and back on the many, many of us who suffer in the very deepest parts of ourselves, uncomforted and wounded by the depth of the self-loathing that shame brings.

It is distressing, as I mentioned early in my story, to have intrusive thoughts of molesting a child go through your head. It is distressing, also, to have intrusive sexual thoughts about another person, whether that is someone of the opposite gender who is not your spouse or of someone who is the same gender. With Scrupulosity, those quite often include sexual thoughts about religious leaders such as a pastor or Sunday school teacher. The embarrassment and horror a person with Religious Scrupulosity experiences with these thoughts cannot be overstated, especially for those of us raised in churches in which sex was only mentioned in the context of sin and lust. Add to that the completely involuntary sexual arousal that can accompany those thoughts, and the stage is set for deep shame, gender attraction confusion, and fears that one is a sexual pervert. It can lead to avoiding people or situations which trigger those thoughts and responses. We are convinced that because those thoughts cross our minds, then we must want to do what the thoughts suggest, and therefore we are evil, adulterous, sexual perverts.

I cannot imagine anything more distressing, though, than the unwanted, intrusive sexual thoughts about God which I experienced as part of Scrupulosity. For me, the most frequent triggers were reading my Bible and praying—the foundations of Christian discipline and practice. I also struggled with blasphemous thoughts during those activities, but far worse were the unwanted, intrusive sexual thoughts about God. This happened frequently when I would try to express my love for God, as well.

As soon as those thoughts would happen, I would immediately try to shut them down. My old standby verse: "Purge me with hyssop, and I will be clean. Wash me and I will be whiter than snow," was my plea. I would sing songs or quote Scriptures to try to stop the thoughts. But, like the proverbial "pink elephant in the room" which we are not supposed to think about, the more I would try to ward off the thoughts, the more often they plagued me. Heartbroken, I would decide I wasn't going to think about God anymore because I could not bear to think of the God I love like that. It would not be long, though, before I would be plagued by thoughts that I was going to go to hell because I (thought I) did not have a relationship with God.

I go often in my mind back to the four-year-old child I was when I gave my heart to Jesus. The love I had for God was deep and sweet, and my love for God, through all the years of abuse and mental illness never went away. It was devastating for me to have that love seemingly tarnished and destroyed by thoughts I did not even want to have!

Those were awkward conversations—to say the least—to have with my pastors, but being driven to confess by the Scrupulosity, I did share this with a few of them. How I wish they had known about Religious Scrupulosity OCD! For the most part, I have avoided those pastors due to the embarrassment of the things I shared. In some ways, I feel like I unnecessarily exposed myself. Learning gentleness with myself over this is still a work in progress. Part of what drives me to share my story is the desire to spare others from the shame and embarrassment that is part of Scrupulosity.

A few years before I was diagnosed with Religious Scrupulosity OCD, I was in the midst of a particularly dark and unhealthy place mentally—partially due to some circumstances I will share in a later chapter—and my Scrupulosity was the worst it had been since my early twenties. It was summertime, and for many Christians who grew up in the church, that meant camp meeting time. For lots of people, camp meeting is the highlight of their year, a time to get together with friends they seldom see and to be renewed spiritually. Camp meeting for me, though, was one long trigger. If there was ever a concerted time that reminded me I was a complete failure spiritually, it was camp meeting. Being in a large congregation where others are experiencing God's presence—either in a glorious way or even in conviction—while I am sitting there either unmoved or fighting intrusive thoughts was always one of the most jarringly humiliating experiences.

That year was even worse than normal. Not only was I not in a good place mentally and emotionally, but the preaching was particularly triggering to me. The evangelist was very focused on healing, and while he spent a good amount of time recounting stories of physical healing and how he was gifted in mediating that healing, he also talked a lot about healing from sexual addiction, mental illness, and depression. I do not exaggerate when I say that his preaching was very guilt-inducing as he made healing out to be something we could claim and attain by faith and that if we were not being healed, it was our own fault. At the end of his very long message one day, he began to give the invitation to come to the altar for healing. He practically guaranteed that we would be delivered from depression, anxiety, and mental illness if we would just let him pray with us. I was all in! I was miserable and wanted so badly to be healed, and I was desperate enough that I would have even gone forward to the altar and knelt, something which was difficult mentally and emotionally for me to do. Dozens of people from all over the congregation were going forward until the altars and aisles were filled with people wanting healing. Just as I was preparing myself to go forward, though, the evangelist proceeded to say that under no circumstances were we to come forward unless God was speaking to us to do so.

"Well," I thought, "that leaves me out." I was not able to sense God's presence or voice, so healing was obviously not available for me. I was emotionally devastated. My anguish at having had healing held out to me and then snatched back so unceremoniously crushed my soul. Seldom have I felt more intensely the depth of my own unworthiness and unacceptability to God. I left the tabernacle sobbing and could not stop. Seeking out my pastor afterward, in broken words, I poured out my humiliation and sorrow over my "lack" of relationship with God. My pastor patiently helped pick up the shattered pieces and tried to help me see things from a different angle. (It helped that he himself had serious qualms about the evangelist's message and methods.) While still feeling defeated and hopeless, I was at least able to move forward again.

Due to responsibilities at home, we had to leave camp meeting a day early, Saturday instead of Sunday. We attended service at our own church on Sunday morning. Our pastor, who also functioned as our worship leader, was still at camp, so one of our young adult leaders led us in worship that morning. His style and personality were much different from those I usually connect well with, and I truly did not care for his voice, but because he was leading, I was determined to be a good follower. As I have mentioned before, demonstrative worship—raising hands, for instance—is not something I am comfortable with, and it can be triggering. That morning, though, our leader had us all stand, and because the song said to raise your hands and turn around, he instructed us to do so. Being very committed to the mutual submission of corporate worship, I reluctantly offered it up to God as an act of obedience, and when those phrases came up in the song, I put my hands in the air.

And, Jesus put His face into my hands.

It was just for a moment, but as real as if I held my husband's or child's face in my hands, I held the face of God, and time stood still. The love and tenderness radiating from His face were breathtakingly beautiful! It was as intimate a moment as I have ever experienced in my life. The humility of God in Christ letting me hold His face as one holds the face of only the closest and dearest relatives and friends still fills me with awe and wonder. For much of my life, I was afraid that my "uncleanness," my sinfulness, made me despicable and unworthy of God's love. I thought that somehow my sinfulness would sully God. Like the woman in Scripture who, due to a bleeding disorder was considered unclean and whose touch made any she touched unclean, I had suffered the aloneness and humiliation of my "disorder." In addition, I had felt like my own love was worthless trash, not good enough for humans, let alone for God.

In that moment as I held the face of Jesus, I knew myself to be loved, but even more than that, I knew Jesus not only accepted my love, but it meant something to Him. His face was filled with the delighted awareness of one who knows they are loved. I did that! I brought delight to Jesus through my love for Him. My love for Him was enough. It was accepted as the most priceless, prized treasure, and as if it came from the holiest saint—from Christ's beloved. He did not experience my touch to His face as dirty or impure; He saw my heart and my deep love for Him, and He absolutely radiated delight over my love for Him. A more holy moment than that is hard to imagine.

Once again, God used something familiar to me within my religious tradition—the raising of hands in praise—to bring healing. Where shame and guilt had made that type of demonstrative worship difficult for me, God recognized and used my obedience as an occasion to minister healing to me and in so doing, redeemed an avenue of worship. The grace and creativity of God in being able to reveal Godself to me despite the difficulties of mental illness continues to fill me with awe and worship. At so many points along my journey, God was working in ways I never could have imagined, bringing healing bit by bit to my life. God knows so well what will provide the most help and insight to individuals and is a master at reaching through the darkest darkness of our minds to shine the light of hope. Even before being diagnosed with Scrupulosity OCD, God was working on some of the most difficult aspects of it, the self-loathing and the harm that the Thought-Action Fusion caused in my being able to love and be loved by God.

As we move on to the next chapter, there is one final aspect of Religious Scrupulosity OCD I wish to cover before we turn to how pastors and other religious leaders can help and support those in their care whom they suspect have Scrupulosity. I call it the idol of certainty.

Chapter 6

Challenge #3: The Idol of Certainty

Sitting around the table of our abuse survivor's group, we took the paper our leader handed us. On it was a simple outline of a face with no features or color. Each person was to draw a representation of how we think God views us. After finishing, we would go around and let each person who wanted to tell us about their picture. Out of the corner of my eye, I caught glimpses of what others were drawing. Some had beautiful flowers, some were full of color and vibrancy. Reaching for the white crayon, I proceeded to color over the black outline on my paper, methodically covering each part.

When it was my turn to share, the ladies in my group were surprised to hear what I said. They were expecting me to say the white represented the work of Jesus in my life to make me holy. They thought it meant I saw myself as clean and pure in God's sight.

"I think I am invisible to God," I said. "I don't think God sees me at all."

Spiritual abuse and Scrupulosity had robbed me of more than just my mental health; it had robbed me of the ability to experience God's presence and informed me that I was too sinful for God to have anything to do with. In addition, when I was growing up, my dad employed the "silent treatment" on those he was mad at. He was an expert at it. If my dad was angry at you, you simply did not exist! I remember as a child thinking maybe I really was invisible and looking down at my body to be sure it was still there. It is no surprise, then, that between the silent treatment and the teaching about God not abiding in the presence of sin I came to believe I was invisible to God. God's seeming absence in my life confirmed this over and over. Although I knew the Bible teaches that God loves me, because of my inability to know with certainty that I was saved from sin, I somehow thought God's love was tied to my salvation, and therefore did not know with any sense of certainty that God loved me. This left me with an intense feeling of abandonment and terror and led to many of the compulsions I used to try to find certainty in my relationship with God.

One of the most observed aspects of obsessive-compulsive disorder—no matter the type—is what psychologists call the "intolerance of uncertainty." People with OCD, "…believe that they can (and must) obtain proof [of whatever their particular concern is], and consequently experience a great deal of anxiety and distress when they realize that no such proof exists."[9] A person with a hand-washing compulsion, for instance, will wash and wash their hands trying to arrive at certainty that their hands are clean. It truly is impossible to know for certain that one's hands are completely free from all germs. With Scrupulosity, in particular, people "have trouble accepting the

---

9. Scrupulosity: A cognitive-behavioral analysis and implications for treatment; Jonathan S. Abramowitz, Ryan J. Jacoby; Journal of Obsessive-Compulsive and Related Disorders 3 (2014) 140-149.

inherent uncertainty of particular religious beliefs and doctrines (e.g., 'God loves me') ... Other members of their religion accept these beliefs and doctrines on faith; but it as if those with scrupulosity have *lost their faith in faith*."[10]

The intolerance of uncertainty in Religious Scrupulosity OCD is manifested in several different ways. Much like a person who obsessively washes their hands to be completely certain their hands are clean ("maybe if I wash one more time...") people with Scrupulosity will repeat religious rituals over and over. For example, I had to be certain I had read every word in the Bible, so I would read and reread portions to make sure I had not missed a single word. If I yawned in the middle of the Lord's Prayer, I would start at the beginning to make sure I said it correctly. Repeating the same prayers, crossing oneself again and again, and confessing the same sin multiple times are all examples of this. The anxiety caused by the uncertainty of having done things correctly builds and builds until the person repeats the activity "just to be sure."

For those who have compulsions to tell others about God, they will do this every time someone's name crosses their minds or if the thought to do so crosses their minds when they see a stranger, even if it means missing work or taking them repeatedly away from their daily responsibilities. They are afraid of missing God's will or of being disobedient; if that person dies and goes to hell, they think it will be their fault. When the scrupulous person feels compelled to pray with someone or for someone, they do not dare ignore that feeling, even when doing so interrupts other important activities. The uncertainty of when God is prompting a person to do something and when it

---

10. Ibid

is the person's own compulsion is remedied by always doing the compulsion. Quite often with Scrupulosity, discerning God's direction is extremely difficult because the compulsions frequently mirror important aspects of one's actual religious obligations. Telling others about Jesus, praying with and for others, testifying of God's faithfulness, and giving money to those in need—all are foundational to living out our Christian faith. A person with Scrupulosity, though, often cannot discern when it is an act of obedience and when it is the drive of Scrupulosity. To deal with the anxiety caused by the intolerance of uncertainty, they do the compulsion, no matter how out of step it is with the rest of their lives.

Another aspect involves whether one has sinned, is sinning, or will sin. Individuals with Scrupulosity fear sinning. They must know beyond a shadow of a doubt if something is sinful or not. As mentioned elsewhere, there are no gray areas, only black and white, sin or not sin, right or wrong. "Follow your own conscience" is tantamount to telling us to go sin because many of us have been so deeply shaped by Scriptures like, "The heart is deceitful above all things, and desperately wicked: who can know it?" (Jeremiah 17:9 KJV). We do not trust ourselves to know right from wrong; that must come from outside of us through religious authorities. Seeking reassurance from those around us is not about seeking their wisdom but about finding certainty.

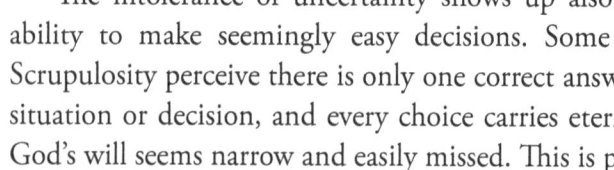

The intolerance of uncertainty shows up also in the inability to make seemingly easy decisions. Some who have Scrupulosity perceive there is only one correct answer to every situation or decision, and every choice carries eternal weight. God's will seems narrow and easily missed. This is perhaps one of the most paralyzing aspects of Scrupulosity OCD.

In the sense that theologically I am a Wesleyan, it seems ironic I would struggle with "God's perfect will" as much as I did. It was not that I believed God had one set, pre-determined path I was supposed to walk, and I somehow miraculously had to find it. It was more that every choice was between sin and not sin, right and wrong. It is hard to explain, but for me, it was not about finding which choice or choices God wanted me to make. Instead, it was that if I was a sinful person, then I could make sinful choices that could send me to hell.

Take the can of green beans, for instance. As I stood there contemplating which can of green beans to buy, I honestly did feel there was only one correct answer, one right can of green beans. Do I buy the cheapest because that would be financially responsible? But, the cheapest sometimes has pieces of vine in it. Do I buy a specific name brand? Perhaps that company supports something immoral; if I buy their products, (my logic told me) I am participating in their immorality. Do I buy my husband's favorite? That is what a kind wife would do. I had to weigh all the possibilities to figure out which can a true Christian would buy. Do I wear purple socks today? Perhaps purple is the color of pride. Maybe I'm trying to attract undue attention. And so on it goes.

As a parent, this made the most mundane questions from my children into significant issues. "May we go outside and play?" my children would ask, and suddenly I would be filled with panic trying to decide the correct answer. "What's for dinner?" could cause me to shut down entirely as all the possibilities were sorted through my mind in an attempt to find which one was the "correct" choice. Again, it was not that I thought God had one predetermined choice that miraculously I had to figure out. It was that the choices themselves were somehow sinful or not sinful, and as a Christian, I had to know for sure that the choice I made was a choice a Christian should make.

For me, personally, and for many others, the most paralyzing aspect of Scrupulosity is the need for certainty in my relationship with God. This is what plagued me beyond anything else. I needed to know for sure I was saved. Religious leaders contributed much to my angst in this area: "You will know that you know that you know (you are saved)" was (and still is) an often-spoken statement in sermons and religious conversations. For most of my life, though, I did not know. The seemingly elusive "witness of the Spirit" did not happen for me, or more correctly, did not happen in ways my mind could recognize due to the Scrupulosity. This tormented me! Because I lacked certainty in my relationship with God, I could not accept that I was saved. I would beg God to save me, to give me the assurance that I was saved. Barring that assurance, I thought I must not be saved and lived with such intense fears of dying and going to hell that I became mentally paralyzed.

Those who have never experienced the lack of assurance cannot begin to understand how devastating and demoralizing it is. To then have blame heaped on top with accusations that we must be holding out on God, or we must have some secret sin we have not confessed, or we have not done all we can to show God we are sincere brings on tortuous self-examination to find and fix our broken selves so God can forgive us and take us in.

I also had no assurance of God's love. It was not that I thought God did not love me—I knew God was a loving God. Going back to my story at the beginning of this chapter, I thought I was so sinful that God could not even look at me, that God did not even think about me, let alone love me. I was invisible to God. The shame-filled ways the "gospel" had been presented to me left no room for God's love. Yes, "God so loved the world…" (John 3:16), so in general God loved me, but I did not think God loved *me* individually. I remember many times receiving Communion and the pastor would say, "Debi, you know God loves you, right?" Inside, I answered with a resounding "NO!"

Communion—the Lord's Supper, Eucharist—is indeed another area of great angst for many, even those who do not suffer from Scrupulosity. For many, many years, I would not receive Communion because I was not completely certain I was saved. The church of my childhood had focused so strongly on not eating "unworthily" ("For he that eateth and drinketh unworthily, eateth and drinketh damnation to himself...." 1 Corinthians 11:29 KJV) that I lived in terror that if I had not properly asked forgiveness for my sins, I would heap damnation on myself if I partook of Communion. The Lord's Supper was certainly not a means of grace to me! This is true of many, many people who have Scrupulosity. For those who do manage to receive Communion, it is quite often preceded by intense self-scrutiny, repentance, and praying some sort of "sinner's prayer" to make sure one's heart is right with God first. Like the person who repeatedly washes their hands to make certain they are clean, they must make sure they are "clean" of sin before participating in the Lord's Supper.

We are taught, of course, that "the just shall live by faith," and that is certainly true! One of the reasons why I titled this chapter "The Idol of Certainty" is because the need for certainty can replace faith in the life of a person with Scrupulosity. This is true for others as well. Many people insist on certainty in their walk with Christ. We are often taught that doubt is the opposite of faith; so if we are uncertain, then we are told we are doubting, which is the same as not living by faith. Doubt, however, is NOT the opposite of faith! Without the possibility of doubt, there cannot be the possibility of faith. For instance, we cannot prove with empirical evidence that God exists. God's existence must be taken by faith. Forgiveness and reconciliation likewise cannot be proven. There is no proof we can lay out on a table and point at to show that we know we are forgiven. We rely on Scriptures such as, "If we confess our sins, he is faithful and just and will forgive us our sins and purify us from all unrighteousness." (1 John 1:9 NIV).

Early in my quest to answer "Yes" to Jesus' question about wanting to get well, I chose to rely on this Scripture. I knew if I had confessed my sins, then God had promised to forgive me. If there was one thing I did not doubt, it was God's faithfulness, so I chose to "live by faith." Would you believe I was ridiculed for this? I was told that I was "settling for less" than God had for me. If I did not have assurance I was saved, they would say, then I probably was not. Imagine being told that living by faith was "less than"!

A significant step on my journey toward wholeness happened a couple of years after the ladies' retreat I mentioned in Chapter 4, but before I was diagnosed with Religious Scrupulosity OCD. The worship pastor at the Church of the Nazarene we were attending was leading the church through Lent. While I am drawn to all things liturgical and enjoy closely following the church calendar, Lent was often difficult for me due to the Scrupulosity OCD. I would start with such high ambitions to use those forty days to draw closer to God and reorient my life around Him. I would usually pick a couple of things from which to fast, such as Dr. Pepper and computer games. My intent would be that anytime I wanted a Dr. Pepper or wanted to play a computer game, I would use that as a reminder that my dependence is on God. Generally, I would start strong, but at some point, I would forget and drink a Dr. Pepper or play a game. The guilt this would induce was terrible! I would feel like I had broken a vow to God and that maybe deep inside, I did not want to draw near to God; perhaps I was not even a Christian, is what my mind would say to me.

That particular year, our worship pastor was helping us lean into the confession and humility of Lent, so one Sunday morning, he requested that we kneel to pray during the pastoral prayer. Kneeling was not our usual posture. For me, kneeling for prayer was intensely difficult and something I avoided. It was often a trigger for Scrupulosity OCD thoughts, specifically thoughts that demons might attack me while I am trying to pray or intrusive sexual thoughts about God. Ultimately, though, I am a conformist and do not lightly defy those in religious authority over me, so offering the kneeling up to God as an act of obedience, I knelt.

Immediately I saw Jesus in front of me. I always hesitate when telling this story because my church tradition does not often talk about visions, or when they do, they are often surrounded with skepticism or suspicion; however, I do not know another way of explaining what I saw but to say it was a vision. Jesus was standing there before me as I knelt there, and his hands were outstretched to me. I went and took his hands in my own hands and noticed the scars on his palms. I began to trace around one of them with my finger then realized the scar was in the shape of my name. My name was engraved on the palm of his hand! Jesus then took that hand with my name on it and placed it over his heart as if I was the most precious person in the world to him. Reaching out, he drew me to his chest, and as I rested against him, he wrapped his arm around me; the sleeve of his snow-white garment covering me entirely down to my feet. Then, placing his hands on my shoulders, Jesus drew my forehead to his lips and placed a sealing kiss on my forehead. Never had I known such love and security! Just as our pastor ended his prayer, Jesus disappeared, but what had happened inside my heart was life-changing!

Many readers will no doubt recognize the symbolism in what I saw. From Isaiah 49:15-16, "Can a mother forget the baby at her breast and have no compassion for the child she has borne? Though she may forget, I will not forget you! See, I have engraved you on the palms of my hands...." While I recognize this particular Scripture was written about Israel, I still believe God used a symbol I would recognize in order to show me how He feels about me. A scar is permanent; a person carries it with them wherever they go. God was saying to me through the symbolism of a scar that Jesus knows me and loves me, and would never leave me or forsake me. God was also saying that Jesus' death on the cross was enough for me. ==I was included in the forgiveness He offered.==

What do we do when something touches us deeply? Quite often, we put our hands over our hearts. It signifies a deep emotional connection. When Jesus put His name-engraved hand over His heart, He was showing me the depth of His love for me. I have never felt more seen and cherished than I felt at that moment!

While my theological tradition affirms that Jesus doesn't just "cover" my sins like one covers someone with a garment, but indeed cleanses it away, still I recognized the symbolism of Jesus' robe covering me as saying that my sins were forgiven and I was washed clean. Not only that, but I also felt secure in Jesus' embrace.

Finally, Jesus placing a sealing kiss on my forehead completely transfixed me. For my whole life, I had lived in fear of the "mark of the beast," that horrible seal that would doom me forever to hell. I was terrified of that mark. Churches did a great job of letting us know to avoid that at all costs! However, mentioned multiple times in Revelation, as well, are beautiful verses that say those who belong to the Lamb will also be marked on their forehead with His mark. As Christians, we bear the mark, the seal of Christ, and Jesus was saying to me that He had sealed me as His own.

Even as I write this, I am again in awe of how God was able to reach beyond my own inability to perceive the witness of the Spirit and find a way to speak truth into my darkness. In the midst of my gratefulness, though, I am keenly aware there are others who have not experienced that assurance, and I feel deeply the grief of that. In sharing my own story, I do not in any way want to add to the burden they carry. For nearly forty years, I lived without assurance. Even now I have no felt sense of assurance most of the time. I have brief moments of time—like during the beautiful vision I just shared—when I "know that I know that I know," but most of the time I still live by faith that God has done what God said God would do. I am thankful for this and other memories of times when God was able to help my mind clearly experience the assurance of the Spirit. I replay those in my mind during times of deep uncertainty. I refuse, however, to let certainty become the goal. Living by faith is not "less than."

Recently (I think maybe in a Sunday school class) we were talking about the story of God's covenant with Abram

(Abraham) in Genesis 15. "After this, the word of the LORD came to Abram in a vision: ... He took him outside and said, 'Look up at the sky and count the stars—if indeed you can count them.' Then he said to him, 'So shall your offspring be.' Abram believed the LORD, and he credited it to him as righteousness." (Genesis 15:1, 5-6). We all know the story well, how Abram then went and prepared the animals for the covenant, laying them out and scaring off the birds. Then, in verse 12 it says, "As the sun was setting, Abram fell into a deep sleep."

"As the sun was setting...." Have you ever noticed that statement in light of the earlier one, "Look up at the sky and count the stars—if indeed you can count them," and considered that maybe it was daytime when God told Abram to do that? The setting sun happened *after* God told Abram to count the stars. If—and obviously we do not know for sure because it was a vision—but, if God had shown Abram the daytime sky and told him to count the stars, what a meaningful illustration it would have been to Abram (and to us!) of how even when we do not see any indication of a promise being fulfilled, it is still there, just not visible.

That, to me, is what living by faith means. I may not have some feeling of assurance, and I might not believe in myself, but I believe in the One who is always faithful and always fulfills promises. Learning to keep my eyes off myself and my feelings and on the trustworthiness and faithfulness of God helps me not get caught back up in the trap of seeking certainty where there is none. My inability to experience certainty does not negate God's faithfulness. Seeking the Person of the Holy Spirit instead of seeking an experience helps avoid the danger of making certainty into an idol.

In the next chapter as I begin to discuss how to minister to a person with Religious Scrupulosity OCD, I will talk more about the danger—yes, *danger*—of pastors, religious leaders, or even family offering assurance to a person with Scrupulosity. That is one of the ways that certainty can become an idol for people who struggle. When assurance becomes the end-all, be-all, the quest for it can become all-consuming and worsen Scrupulosity. In fact, letting go of the demand for certainty is the only way for a person to begin to deal with Scrupulosity.

Part III

Helps and Hindrances to
Healing from Scrupulosity

Chapter 7

The Call to Bind Up the Brokenhearted

"The Spirit of the Sovereign Lord is on me,
because the Lord has anointed me
to proclaim good news to the poor.
He has sent me to bind up the brokenhearted,
to proclaim freedom for the captives
and release from darkness for the prisoners,
to proclaim the year of the Lord's favor
and the day of vengeance of our God,
to comfort all who mourn,
and provide for those who grieve in Zion—
to bestow on them a crown of beauty
instead of ashes,
the oil of joy
instead of mourning,
and a garment of praise
instead of a spirit of despair.
(Isaiah 61:1-3a)

With these beautiful words, Jesus began His formal ministry on earth. I have often been struck by the realization that Jesus did not just come to deal with the sin in a person's life. He did not just come to heal bodies. Instead, Jesus, from the very outset of His ministry, focused on the emotionally hurting and brought healing to the brokenness inside. As the Church—Jesus' hands and feet to a hurting world—we are also called to "bind up the brokenhearted." However, we must do it with wisdom and understanding. In the case of ministering to those with Scrupulosity, it is easy to stray from being helpful into doing more harm. This chapter aims to provide the groundwork for pastors and other religious leaders, as well as family and friends, to minister effectively to those with Scrupulosity.

The starting point for dealing with someone with Scrupulosity—really, for any person dealing with a mental illness—is compassion. There is no adequate way to convey how excruciatingly painful Scrupulosity is to the sufferer. Meet us with compassion. Cry with us over the pain we are in. We are very aware that our thinking is off. We are also very aware that we make people uncomfortable, and they see us as "needy." We have seen our pastors and even our friends try to avoid us when we go to them one more time for assurance and help. In the same way that you would not turn away from someone who is bruised and bleeding, please do not turn away from us. Our wounds are invisible, but they are there. When we see the frustration in your eyes, our shame increases, so start with a posture of compassion. I will never forget sharing my story with one of my pastors and watching the tears pour down his face. It brought some light into my darkness.

Additionally, recognize that the person with Scrupulosity is almost certainly not spiritually stunted or ignorant. Many of us have vast portions of Scripture committed to memory and have probably read the Bible even more than our pastors. We know the doctrines of our particular church because we have spent hours making sure we line up in every conceivable way. Not to be forgotten, too, is the fact of God's faithfulness in the lives of believers. It is likely that even though those with Scrupulosity struggle with assurance of their relationship with God, they are growing in their faith. The Holy Spirit is faithful to work even when we cannot see it or identify it.

An important question, then, is how to determine if a person is merely conscientious or if they might have Scrupulosity. Of course, unless you are a doctor or counselor, you cannot diagnose. There are, however, a few things to look for.

One of the significant things about Scrupulosity is that there is a constant need for confession and assurance. In the same way that hand-washing works for a person with a germ obsession, assurance works for those with Scrupulosity. The author of an article on spiritual direction for those who suffer from Scrupulosity expresses it succinctly:

> Someone seeking spiritual direction who is in the throes of scrupulous anxiety will appear scared, desperate, unusually rigid and difficult to persuade, and possibly ashamed. Individuals in this situation are scared because their minds are confronting them with a fear of damnation that is so intense they think it must carry weight. They are afraid that if they don't receive reassurance from someone with religious "authority" (often a minister or spiritual director), they will go crazy or have a nervous breakdown as a result of the anxiety. Driven by this fear, these spiritual directees are desperate to

hear the spiritual director say the right words that will relieve their suffering.

Another characteristic that spiritual directors may notice is that scrupulous individuals can sometimes be "cured" of their anxiety almost instantaneously when the spiritual director offers the right word of reassurance or performs a requested ritual. When this happens, it is because the reassurance or ritual has accomplished the necessary "compulsion" to relieve the sufferer's "obsession." The correct compulsion [assurance] works on the sufferer's mind like a drug, relieving the overwhelming anxiety and inducing a euphoric sense of relief. The spiritual directee is grateful, the spiritual director feels successful, and all appears well—until the next obsession hits, with an even stronger urge to apply to the spiritual director for relief. This dynamic provides temporary "quick fixes" to the sufferer's anxiety but does not move them any further along the road to recovery. In addition, it can quickly lead to dependency and the souring or rupture of the relationship.[11]

To summarize from this, then, look for:

- Desperation and fear. A merely conscientious person can still derive peace and joy from their faith. A person trying to justify sin will not have the same sense of desperation and fear.

---

[11]. https://www.ocdmassachusetts.org/2014/06/25/ocd-scrupulosity-spiritual-direction-through-the-stages-of-recovery/

- The continual need for reassurance. A conscientious person does not necessarily need assurance. Their conscientiousness can be part of what brings them joy and peace in their relationship with God. A person with Scrupulosity needs reassurance (certainty) for survival.
- Relief of anxiety when offered assurance.

The obsessions and compulsions that plague individuals with Scrupulosity can also be indicators. If a person shares concerns about unwanted or intrusive thoughts they are having, for instance, that would be a reason to suspect Scrupulosity.

When it becomes apparent that a person may suffer from Scrupulosity, it is important to refer them for professional help. The measures pastors and spiritual leaders usually employ to help those with doubts will *not* work with Scrupulosity but can instead do more harm.

In conjunction with referring to professional help, it is essential to set and maintain good boundaries with the person. This is for your sanity and safety, of course, but it is also vital for the health and welfare of the person to whom you are ministering.

One of my pastors was an exceptionally compassionate man. He was an incredible pastor with a shepherd's heart. Shortly after we moved to our new military base and started attending the church he pastored, I went to him needing some assurance. He was so compassionate and kindly reassured me of God's love and that I could trust God. The instant relief from my anxiety was wonderful. It was not long, though, until all the doubts and fears were back, so back to my pastor I went. He was committed to helping me find rest in God, so he once again reassured me. Relief. Then back again. He told me I could email, call, or text him any time, so in addition to the church phone number and email address, he gave me his cell phone number. At first, I only texted or emailed him a couple of times a month, but as the anxiety grew, I began to text him more frequently. He always faithfully answered back, assuring me. Soon, I was texting him several times a week, then every day, and then several times a day. As he answered each one, rather than my anxiety lessening, it escalated until it became constant. For the first time in many, many years, the anxiety drove me back to self-harming behaviors I thought I had left far behind. The repeated obsession, a spike of anxiety, and then the resolution through assurance set up a vicious cycle. At one point, he and his wife were going to take a vacation, and I completely fell apart, practically screaming at him that he could not do this to me. Thankfully, I started back into counseling shortly after that, and the counselor (who was also my pastor's counselor) put a stop to that. It was a devastating time for me. I was cut off from my primary source of assurance and, therefore, relief.

I want to reiterate that this was a wonderful pastor, a genuinely compassionate man of God. It was his compassion without good boundaries, though, which ended up causing me more harm. Had he been educated about Scrupulosity, I believe he would have handled it differently, and I might have received help sooner.

Compassion with good boundaries, then, is essential, and why referring to counseling is so important. However, counselors who are not educated about Scrupulosity are not exempt from the same pitfalls. One of my counselors made the same mistake as my pastor, allowing me to become far too dependent on him for assurance, thus causing an increase in my Scrupulosity. As you encourage someone to seek counseling, they must convey to the counselor that they suspect Religious Scrupulosity OCD. Many, like I was, are in counseling for other mental health issues but do not mention their "spiritual issues" because they take those to their pastor. Alerting their counselor to the possibility of having Scrupulosity can help the counselor with diagnosis and treatment. The reality is that not every counselor is knowledgeable about Scrupulosity, so it may be necessary for the person to seek out a counselor who specializes in Obsessive-Compulsive Disorders.

Do not be surprised if the person with Scrupulosity is resistant to counseling. Often a person with Scrupulosity will be afraid that by agreeing they have a mental illness, they may be deceived by Satan into not taking responsibility for their sinfulness. You will likely experience significant pushback from them. You will have to patiently keep pointing them toward the help they need while also maintaining healthy boundaries around the care you can provide.

From a psychological perspective, Religious Scrupulosity is treatable. While being a more challenging mental illness to treat because it involves the fear of eternal damnation, it does respond to a combination of treatments. First, medications can help decrease anxiety, allowing a person to work on the issues causing the anxiety. Medications, alone, generally do not cure a person with OCD. A type of treatment that is very effective is called Exposure and Response Prevention, which essentially exposes a person to something which would cause an increase in anxiety but does not let them perform the ritual to relieve the anxiety. Long before I knew about Scrupulosity, my counselors used Exposure and Response Prevention with me to work on the Agoraphobia and other OCD issues I had. The process of leaving my house and working up to going places by myself used this approach. The more I purposefully exposed myself to the things I was afraid of, the less they bothered me. ==This "learning to live with the uncomfortable" is an integral part of the healing process.== When I began to work on the Scrupulosity, for instance, as I read Scripture, I would not allow myself to go back and read over a section if I thought I had missed a word. Instead of praying the Lord's Prayer repeatedly to make sure I said every word, I would say it one time and live with the uncomfortableness of not knowing if I had said it correctly. Over time, this helped eliminate the rise in anxiety that led to the compulsive behavior. It is similar to how allergy shots decrease the body's immune response, allowing a person with allergies to be around allergy triggers without their body responding. By not doing compulsions, the brain is retrained not to react when faced with Scrupulous thoughts. ERP can be highly distressing, though, so lots of encouragement through the process is needed.

Your involvement with that person does not necessarily end with your referring them, however. Often, a counselor will invite pastors to be a part of the process by helping the counselor and the counselee know the standard expected requirements of the person's faith tradition. In addition, a pastor can provide the assurance—this time in a helpful way—that the treatment for Scrupulosity may require doing things the person may think are sinful but are, in fact, necessary to recover from Scrupulosity. For instance, a person with Scrupulosity may be allowed only to read five verses instead of five chapters from the Bible in a day. The pastor can assure the person that this is perfectly acceptable. Or, they may be required to purposefully allow a thought to form in their mind without repeating any Scripture verses or prayers to ward it off. The pastor can assure them that it is necessary to retrain their brain, although it is uncomfortable. A trusted pastor's involvement with the counselor can help the person with Scrupulosity dare to pursue treatment.

A word of caution is necessary here, however. It is very easy to slip over into providing unhealthy assurance in the process of trying to help. Some counselors discourage the involvement of pastors and religious leaders for this very reason. Based on what a counselor feels is best for their client, it may be necessary for those close to the person struggling with Scrupulosity not to allow them to consult you about their doubts and fears. It is a tricky distinction to make and one which should be made both prayerfully and in conjunction with the counselor. Honesty with the person with Scrupulosity about why you are pulling back is also necessary. When my pastor told me he was pulling back from interacting with me, he was kind and gentle, assuring me I had done nothing wrong. Although I was devastated and struggled, in the long run, his setting and maintaining good boundaries with me pushed me towards seeking help appropriately from a counselor. Pulling back does not mean you do not encourage, show compassion or spend time with the individual. A healthy balance of compassion and boundaries is what is needed.

It is easy for family and friends unwittingly to enable a person with Scrupulosity. Often, increasing amounts of time are required by the person to complete their compulsions, and this can cause significant stress within relationships. Suppose a person, for instance, is driven to genuflect over and over at the altar to "get it correct" before they are able to leave the church building. In that case, families are often held captive, waiting for their loved one to complete the compulsion. Families will often say it is easier to do that than not to let the person finish their compulsion.

The International OCD Foundation calls these types of enabling "Family Accommodation Behaviors" and defines them as "things families do that enable OCD symptoms." They provide a helpful list of what this looks like:

- **Participating in the behavior.** You participate in your family member's OCD behavior along with them. Example: You wash your hands whenever they wash their hands.

- **Assisting in avoiding.** You help your family member avoid things that upset them. Example: You do their laundry for them so that it is cleaned the "right" way.

- **Helping with the behavior.** You do things for your family member that lets them do OCD behaviors: Example: You buy large amounts of cleaning products for them.

- **Making changes in family routine.** You alter the way your family usually does things: Example: You change the time of day that you shower or when you change your clothes.

- **Taking on extra responsibilities.** Example: You go out of your way to drive them places when they could otherwise drive themselves.

- **Making changes in leisure activities.** Example: Your family member gets you to not leave the house without them and this affects your interests in movies, dining out, time with friends, etc.

- **Making changes at your job.** Example: You cut back on hours at your job in order to take care of your family member.[12]

These and other similar ways that families, friends, and religious leaders accommodate and enable those with OCD—including those with Scrupulosity OCD—do more harm in the long run. According to extensive research, "Family accommodation is associated with more severe psychopathology and poorer clinical outcomes. … Family accommodation of anxiety disorders represents the intersection of anxiety regulation and close interpersonal behavior as the individual with the anxiety disorder looks to loved ones for aid in avoiding or regulating anxiety and the relatives are propelled to step in and provide accommodation to their distressed loved one."[13]

It is essential for family and friends to learn how to provide support and navigate the pitfalls of accommodation that ultimately are not helpful to the scrupulous person. Seeking the advice of a counselor is always appropriate for learning how to establish healthy boundaries.

Giving spiritual guidance to a person with Scrupulosity can be challenging. However, avoiding the pitfalls of offering assurance when it is not appropriate is only one of the challenges. Compassion and care for the person are necessary, even

---

12. https://iocdf.org/families/
13. https://www.ncbi.nlm.nih.gov/pmc/articles/PMC4895189/

if difficult. It is possible to offer encouragement that can make a difference without unintentionally causing more harm.

My pastors and other religious leaders have provided care for me in various ways. One of the most powerful for me was the simple offer of friendship and affection. Being raised with a deep feeling of unworthiness to take up time and space makes it hard for me to feel like I have any value, especially to those in places of authority, so whenever my pastors or other leaders seek me out (as opposed to me chasing them down for assurance), it is very meaningful. Too often, I have perceived that I make people uncomfortable and have experienced the feeling that they avoid me because they do not know how to help me. When people invite me into their lives, it helps me know I am seen and valued and am not just a burden.

Expressing genuine affection is another way to minister to those with mental illness. Two years ago, a wonderful pastor who was a master at this passed away. I posted the following on Facebook as a tribute to him: "'Be kindly affectionate to one another.' I love this translation of Romans 12:10, especially as I try to put into words what Pastor Tharon Daniels meant to me. Expressed affection is one of the most beautiful and healing aspects of love. To be seen and regarded with 'devoted tenderness' by someone is a gift of immeasurable worth. It seems that overall, this is a lost art. With our social media world, people are wandering around starved for expressions of true affection. Pastor Tharon was an expert at expressing affection. From his constant teasing (a must for a person like me who thrives on teasing and friendly banter) to his endearing nicknames to the gentle tug on my ear as we chatted, his kindly affection brought healing to me. Those of us who are socially awkward know we make people around us uncomfortable, but somehow Pastor

Tharon didn't seem one bit uncomfortable. Instead, the picture he helped me see of myself is that I am lovable, valuable, and cherished. Words cannot begin to convey how that impacted my life. I am so grateful to have known this man."

It can seem challenging to express affection in ways that are not misunderstood in our world. Touch has become almost taboo; pastors and religious leaders must be careful about this, but I still believe there is a place for meaningful, healing touch in our society. Other forms of affection might include something as simple as a smile. I remarked recently to some friends that one of the things I miss most since my parents passed away is that I seldom experience a room lighting up with someone's smile when they see me. Mirroring back to a person their value and worth is powerful.

Because of the way I am wired, one of the most helpful things my pastors have done is to appeal to my intellect. Long before I was diagnosed with Scrupulosity, one of my pastors was meeting with me on a regular basis as I struggled with knowing whether or not I was saved. Pastor David named several more concrete ways I could gain assurance. He mentioned my obvious love for God and my desire to please God. Those were gifts from God. Even though I feared death and the future, we talked about how I nevertheless looked forward to Jesus' return. He then asked if I saw evidence of the Fruit of the Spirit growing in my life. Was I more loving today than a year ago? Did I have more peace and patience today than a year ago? If I did, that was evidence of the presence of God in my life. We do not grow those fruits; the Holy Spirit produces those in us. Their presence means God is at work. He went on to say that if I had trouble seeing them in myself, ask trusted friends and family. These words from so long ago have stuck with me and provided immeasurable comfort and a more concrete way of measuring my growing relationship with God.

In addition, recognizing the countless hours I have spent reading and studying the Bible, theology, and other religious topics, pastors have asked me for help with research and clarification of things they were studying. Including me in this way provided a kind of reassurance that was not harmful.

Getting to know the person with Scrupulosity well enough to know their strengths and then including them in ministry when possible can be a powerful means of healing. Just because a person is mentally ill does not mean they do not have valuable contributions to make. I would also recommend having a backup plan if the person cannot carry through with what they have been tasked to do. Mental illness can be unpredictable, and failing to meet our obligations can cause intense shame. Extending grace and compassion when we do fail helps us move forward.

While it is true that pastors, friends, and family can unwittingly cause more harm by offering assurance and accommodating the compulsions of those with Scrupulosity, it is also true that those with Scrupulosity need a strong support system surrounding them to feel safe enough to pursue counseling and healing. Having pastors and other religious leaders educated in Scrupulosity is essential so that they can recognize it and refer people for counseling and provide appropriate support. This can be especially important for those with Scrupulosity for whom spiritual abuse has contributed to the intensity of their suffering.

One additional note about counseling. There are those for whom the cost of counseling and/or the lack of insurance coverage might be a deterrent to them receiving the help they need. This is another area where the church can come alongside the person, helping them find affordable counseling and assisting with funds to help cover the costs.

As I was doing research for this book, I spoke with several pastors about some of the ways Scrupulosity affects sufferers. Almost every one of them asked an important question. They wanted to know how, as pastors, they unknowingly make things worse for those with Scrupulosity. I so appreciate that question! To answer them, I first addressed how providing assurance can make things worse and the importance of setting healthy boundaries and referring people for counseling when necessary. In addition, I talked to them about how some of the common phrases and practices within churches are experienced differently by those with Scrupulosity. I have mentioned several of those throughout this book, such as how guilt-inducing it is to hear, "you will know that you know that you know you are saved." Things casually mentioned in Sunday School classes and sermons can also become sources of new obsessions and compulsions. In the next chapter, we will look more closely at this, as well as how the issues of culture, politics, and preaching can be difficult for people with Scrupulosity to navigate.

Chapter 8

The Difficulty with Politics, Pandemics, and Preaching

"Where misunderstanding serves others as an advantage, one is helpless to make oneself understood"
—Lionel Trilling (American Critic, Author, and Teacher. 1905-1975)

"I know you think you understand what you thought I said, but I'm not sure you realize that what you heard is not what I meant."
(Variously attributed to Alan Greenspan, Robert McCloskey, and Mark Twain)

Every once in a while, I encounter a book that leaves me frustrated and conflicted. Henry Denker's *Outrage* is one such book. A legal thriller, *Outrage,* presents the story of a man who takes justice into his own hands after the person who raped and murdered his daughter is freed on a technicality. As the heartbroken father stands trial for the murder of the man who stole the life of his daughter, we are challenged by Denker to rethink the very nature of "justice" in the legal system.

What makes Denker's book so challenging for me is the juxtaposition of the need to hold accountable one person who murders while wanting the other "murderer" to go free. It is a moral quandary. For a person like me who wants everything to be clearly right or clearly wrong, it is distressing to encounter ambiguous situations. As much as I dislike life being full of uncertainty, it is, unfortunately, full of it.

As I write this, we are coming out of two long years of dealing with a global pandemic that followed on the heels of several highly contentious years in the political arena. The climate of the last decade has been tumultuous in ways many of us have never before experienced. It often feels as if all our foundations are shifting, and we constantly must reevaluate what we see as accurate and true.

Growing up in politically conservative state, home, and church environments, I was well into my twenties before I realized there were people who claimed to be both Christians and Democrats. Throughout my childhood and early adulthood, I was surrounded by people who shared my same values and political ideologies, so I assumed all Christians believed as I did. In my late twenties, though, I became part of an online Nazarene community that included people from all around the world. I was shocked to discover so many different viewpoints from people whom all identified as Christians, particularly as Nazarenes. Fully engulfed in Scrupulosity at the time, I found myself experiencing deep anxiety as I tried to navigate political and religious ideologies that I had been raised to think of as "liberal" and, therefore, as morally wrong. Hearing from people outside the United States was especially enlightening, though, because it took the conversation totally outside the usual American political party debates and into the realm of considering things based on "the law of love (...love the Lord your God...and love your neighbor as yourself.)." Learning to think for myself in matters of politics and religion was not easy. Being so driven by the Scrupulosity to make sure I did not inadvertently believe something immoral put tremendous stress on my mental health, often leaving me feeling paralyzed. Learning to "live with the uncomfortable" in dealing with Obsessive-Compulsive Disorder, though, gave me a valuable tool as I worked my way through political, social, and spiritual issues.

Despite all that, nothing could have prepared me for the upheaval of the last decade. For me, the most challenging aspect of the political and social climate right now is the lack of unity within the church among Christians. Issues on which there used to be near-universal agreement within the church (or so it seemed) have become issues that now divide churches, communities, and even families. There is support among Christian leaders for all sides of nearly every issue one could bring up. Within the scientific and academic communities, the same can be said.

Take the issues which came up during the Covid-19 pandemic, for example. Something as seemingly straightforward as wearing a mask, for instance, became a significant point of contention. It was intensely bewildering to be told, "If you don't wear a mask, you are unloving," while also being told, "If you wear a mask, you are living in fear and not trusting God." One set of Christians called for people to obey those in authority over them, while another group said that obeying those in leadership was equivalent to taking the mark of the beast. Civil disobedience was encouraged, framed around the civil disobedience of the midwives who defied the Pharoah in Egypt and saved the lives of Hebrew babies. Scripture was being used to justify every conceivable position. Some of the same arguments were used for getting or refusing vaccinations. Doctors and scientists also could be found supporting every side of every issue. Seldom have I seen more Scripture openly used within the political arena, although one could scarcely build a cohesive belief system from the out-of-context, cherry-picking of Scriptures!

It is not the purpose of this book to set individuals straight on various political, social, or religious issues. I can scarcely manage to work my own way through the issues, let alone instruct anyone else! Instead, my intention for including this chapter is to help people understand the current environment's impact on those with mental illness, especially those with Scrupulosity. Yes, everyone has been dramatically impacted by the pandemic and politics of the last few years, but there are particular ways those of us with Scrupulosity struggle.

As you have no doubt realized by now, individuals with Scrupulosity need to know they believe "the truth" and do "what's right." When people fear sinning, they cannot just do their best to do right and hope it is good enough. They must know that it is precisely the right thing to do. More so than many other groups, people with Scrupulosity are prone to holding tenaciously onto positions. As mentioned in Chapter 6, those who have Scrupulosity OCD are very rigid in their thoughts and beliefs because the consequences of what they do and believe are so closely tied to their eternal destiny. Certainty is an absolute must because anything else leaves us open to sinning. The current political and religious climates seem to have no certainty, though, which causes extreme anxiety for those with Scrupulosity and other anxiety disorders.

It is not that we have never faced the contentiousness of politics before. Throughout history, there have been difficult times politically. Somehow, at least for me, these last few years have felt different, however. It feels like religion is now being used as a weapon by all sides. Social media has undoubtedly exacerbated that. Those from one side of an issue will say you cannot be a Christian and do what the other side does. Then the other side will say the same thing about the opposite side. It feels like Jesus is used as a pawn to prop up positions instead of being the foundation upon which we build our beliefs.

One of the most helpful things people can do is stop the guilt-inducing statements that call into question a person's spirituality based on the perception of their political views. We with Scrupulosity fight so hard to believe we are saved; we work diligently to make sure we are doing and believing everything correctly. Having accusations lobbed at us that we are "less than" or even "sinners" because we have come to conclusions different from others can send us spinning back into confusion and obsessions/compulsions to deal with the anxiety. I will never forget sitting in my (Christian) chiropractor's office waiting for my turn to be adjusted as the chiropractor was speaking to the woman on the table next to me about how stupid people were for wearing masks and how they were being deceived by those who were working toward an anti-Christ(!) agenda. Meanwhile, I sat there in my mask, following the government orders for that county and trying hard to be a Christian who loved my neighbor. I was humiliated and crushed in my spirit. What was the right thing to do? It seemed impossible to figure out. It would have been effortless for me to slip back into the

Agoraphobia again and not leave my house for fear that I was not doing the things a Christian should be doing.

Social media, too, was full of friends and family—people I love and look up to and who share my Christian faith—who were stating in no uncertain terms that if people do not believe (fill in the blank), they could not be Christians. And, there I was caught in the middle, not knowing for certain what was right or wrong, not being able to discern what I needed to do or believe, feeling each accusation as a personal blow to my spirit. I wanted so badly to "live a life of love," to live as I thought Jesus wanted me to live, but every time I thought I was, someone would come along and say I was not. During some of the most confusing and frustrating times, I penned these words:

COLLATERAL DAMAGE

We weren't the targets, but we took the strikes—
Thousands of misplaced words—bullets into our hearts.
We weren't the enemy, nor were we friends
No names, no worth,
Just unfortunate souls caught in the crossfire
"Collateral damage"
The "necessary" but tragic sacrifices to win.
Unnoticed we huddled
Bent under the constant blows
Wanting to take sides
But not knowing who were the "good guys."
They all acted like "bad guys,"
Shooting and killing with their words.
Words aimed at the other side
But catching us instead.

> "Collateral Damage"
> "Too bad," they sighed self-righteously.
> "We must prove we are right,
> We must defend God."
> Defend God?
> Who is that Lamb there,
> Strung up on that tree?
> Was He collateral damage, too?

These have been intensely frustrating months for all of us, but having Scrupulosity adds an element of desperation and fear to the conversation. Even as I sit here trying to write this chapter, my fear of being thought ignorant, uninformed, or accused of holding sinful views makes my stomach clench inside, and my anxiety kicks into overdrive. I want to have the "right" views. I want my faith to inform every aspect of my life. It is frustrating beyond belief that all Christians do not have the same opinion on all social issues! I want the Holy Spirit to tell me the same thing the Holy Spirit tells you. Unfortunately, that does not seem to be the way things work.

Over the last couple of years, I have returned to a book I first read about ten years ago, *The Righteous Mind: Why Good People are Divided by Politics and Religion*, by Jonathan Haidt. It has helped me tremendously in understanding how people arrive at their beliefs and why deeply held religious and political views are challenging to change. In addition, research focusing on how our brains respond to information that contradicts our beliefs helps to explain why we continue believing things the way we do. In a fascinating study carried out by neuroscientists at the Brain and Creativity Institute at USC, it was demonstrated that attacks on our politics or religion are perceived by our brain as attacks on our identity. Lead author Jonas Kaplan argues, "Political beliefs are like religious beliefs in the respect that both are part of who you are and important for the social circle to which you belong. To consider an alternative view, you would have to consider an alternative version of yourself."[14] He goes on to say, "The activity in these areas [amygdalae and insular cortex—areas of the brain], which are important for emotion and decision-making, may relate to how we feel when we encounter evidence against our beliefs."[15]

"The amygdala in particular is known to be especially involved in perceiving threat and anxiety," Kaplan added. "The insular cortex processes feelings from the body, and it is important for detecting the emotional salience of stimuli. That is consistent with the idea that when we feel threatened, anxious or emotional, then we are less likely to change our minds." Recent research using MRIs demonstrated this as well.[16] Attacks on a person's identity are met with fierce resistance, so it stands to reason that when our brains are confronted with information—even evidence!—that our beliefs are wrong, our brains tend to hold even tighter to our beliefs rather than change. It is a fascinating phenomenon!

It would be helpful, especially for pastors and those in religious authority, to study the research or read a book like *The Righteous Mind* that helps explain how Christians who believe

---

14. Gersema, E. (2016, December 23). *Hard-Wired: The Brain's circuitry for political belief.* ScienceDaily. Retrieved November 15, 2022, from https://www.sciencedaily.com/releases/2016/12/161223115757.htm (As cited originally in Kaplan, J., Gimbel, S. & Harris, S. Neural correlates of maintaining one's political beliefs in the face of counterevidence. Sci Rep 6, 39589 (2016). https://doi.org/10.1038/srep39589

15. Ibid

16. https://www.nature.com/articles/srep39589.pdf

differently are not being hardheaded or purposely choosing not to obey the Gospel. At the least, maybe it would help all sides to see the damage they do by attacking those with differing beliefs. Challenge ideas, yes, but do so without dehumanizing and destroying people.

There are many political issues people will never agree on, but as Christians, we need to prioritize relationships instead of prioritizing being right. In one sense, it is impossible to separate politics from the Gospel. It has been argued that Jesus was crucified because of politics. It is important to discuss things about social justice, care for the poor and refugees, creation care, race relations, and how to be "pro-life," for example. Our religious beliefs have a bearing on how we approach all these issues. We need to be careful, though, how we throw around statements about who is and is not a Christian or what a Christian would or would not do. It can do incredible damage to those doing their best to figure out how they are supposed to live.

With this in mind, perhaps we could all work toward extending the kind of grace to each other that recognizes that many of us are genuinely doing our best to live holy lives. We are trying to believe the right things. For some of us, myself included, so much of our mental energy is taken up with simply surviving that we struggle to make sense of political and social issues. The process of changing beliefs is slow and difficult. Can we learn to be gracious with each other and trust the presence of the Holy Spirit in each other's lives to help lead us all? I may not have the ability at this moment to focus on a particular issue that is making its way through the news and media, but that does not mean I am being "willfully ignorant," "ignoring the truth," or "not obeying God," etc. If someone is unable to get involved in social and political issues, do not assume they are complacent Christians. Some of them may be working through extremely difficult things in their own lives. Heaping guilt and shame on them for not being like you is damaging, and in the long run, it makes you the ungracious one. Do not let your defense of the position you think is right cause you to treat others with contempt or as less Christian than you.

In a must-read sermon entitled "A Catholic Spirit," John Wesley invites us, "Though we cannot think alike, may we not love alike?"[17] Later in his sermon, he goes on to say, "Every wise man, therefore, will allow others the same liberty of thinking that he desires they should allow him, and will no more insist on their embracing his opinions than he would have them to insist on his embracing theirs. He is patient with those who differ from him, and only asks him with whom he desires to unite in love that single question: 'Is your heart right, as my heart is with your heart?'"[18] I could continue to quote point after point from his sermon, but I will instead invite my readers to read the sermon in its entirety for themselves. If we could all learn to have a Catholic spirit, a spirit that prioritizes relationships over our opinions, perhaps our churches and communities would do less damage to the vulnerable among us who are doing the best they can.

One final area I want to address is how pastors and other leaders can, through their teaching and preaching—and religious people in their discussions—unintentionally add to the burden of a person with Scrupulosity. At the start of this book, I mentioned some of the unhelpful things those who struggle with Scrupulosity and other mental illness have heard in

---

17. https://www.crivoice.org/cathspirit.html
18. Ibid

response to their questions and concerns about their faith and religious duty. There are other more subtle ways damage can be inflicted, however. Because those with Scrupulosity want to live perfectly sinless lives, we are constantly tuned to hear any area where we may be falling short. The conversation my college boyfriend's family had one day comes to mind as a good example. We were discussing how his aunt had died many years before while she was in college, then the conversation turned to how spiritual she was. One of the ways they knew she was so spiritual was because even though she had short, thin hair that would not grow (a terrible thing in that conservative holiness church), she refused to tease or backcomb her hair to make it look thicker. Yes, that is indeed how they knew she was spiritual! My mind grabbed hold of that, and every morning for nearly thirty-five years after that, I had a conversation with myself as I combed and teased my own thinning hair. Every morning I had to justify why it was okay to tease my hair and why it was not a sign of spirituality not to. That conversation had become a compulsion to relieve my anxiety over possibly sinning by teasing my hair. (Interestingly enough, I know there are those out there who would say it was the Holy Spirit convicting me all those years, trying to get me not to be so vain as to backcomb my hair!)

That is perhaps a rather shallow example, but hopefully, you get the idea. It is not just important doctrinal issues that grab our attention. It is anything that could potentially be sinful or less spiritual. Pastors and other religious people can have pet peeves they preach, teach, or discuss without considering how it can affect those who struggle to know God's will. We, in turn, can take on every little thing and make it a spiritual issue.

An issue that perhaps illustrates this in a current way—although with some definite political overtones—is the issue of environmental responsibility. A few years ago, a wonderful chaplain and godly friend was blogging about the different ways her family was trying to care for God's Creation through the things they purchased, such as food and other items with less packaging, and trying not to get anything that contained single-use plastic. This is a responsible way to live, without a doubt. Because she and her family are deeply spiritual people who reflect the love of Jesus so beautifully, and because they did such an excellent job of explaining how this style of living was in line with a holy life, I wanted to emulate them. However, having a brain wired for Scrupulosity, I quickly found myself obsessing over every single item I purchased, wanting to make sure it was eco-friendly, fair trade, local, organic, no plastics, free-range, grass-fed, and so on. Food was already a struggle for me, but now I had to worry about the wrapping, too. When a server at a restaurant would hand me a straw, I would be filled with horrible guilt because that straw could end life here on earth as we know it and send me straight to hell.

I exaggerate a bit for emphasis, but you can perhaps see how overwhelming this sort of thing can be for a person with Scrupulosity. It would possibly be manageable if it were just one issue we had to deal with, but people with Scrupulosity tend to take on issue after issue to make sure they are living holy and sinless lives. This is especially true when the subject is mentioned by a person of religious authority.

It is important to note that I am not at all suggesting this friend should not have been posting about her family's spiritual journey as it intersected with a potentially politically charged issue, or that her view was not "right." Living out our faith in all areas of life is important. My point was that what is a valid issue for Christians to consider can easily become a prison for a person with Scrupulosity. Being mindful of this, I would suggest that religious leaders think about how they can help those who struggle to find balance and extend grace to those who might be working through what they believe. When I shared with my friend what I was experiencing, she graciously did that for me!

Typical daily activities can also be a source of struggle for those with Scrupulosity. Over the last few years, I have seen various advertisements for "Christian diets," with churches sponsoring diet classes. Out of the six people I personally know who have Scrupulosity, four have dealt with an eating disorder, with three requiring significant medical and/or mental health treatment. During research for this book, I have encountered others who struggle with food issues. While sermons about our bodies being the temple of the Holy Spirit used to focus on drug and alcohol use, lately, I have also heard it used to encourage eating "clean," organic, and free-range food. While there may be validity in this view, many people with Scrupulosity, myself included, can become obsessed with every bite that goes into our mouths. For me, personally, food itself is surrounded by feelings of guilt and shame to the point of exhaustion, but it has been helpful to realize the part Scrupulosity plays in these feelings and to continue learning to live this area of my life with grace.

Society's use of foul language can also be a significant trigger for people with Scrupulosity, especially for those raised in a church environment where foul language was considered sinful. (I use the words "foul language" to mean words that have traditionally been considered offensive to society at large, words which would include curses, "taking God's name in vain," ones with sexual connotations or referring to bodily functions, etc. While I recognize there is much controversy over the use of such language, it can be a significant issue for those with Scrupulosity and thus needs to be addressed.) This was—and continues to be—a source of discomfort for me, as well. For most of my life, I was compelled by Scrupulosity OCD to either respond out loud to swear words around me or do a ritual in my mind to "wash away" the contamination of those words. I had to respond because I needed God to know I was not guilty of using those words. Whenever those words would cross my mind, I would quote Scripture to try to banish them. It used to be that church was almost entirely devoid of foul language, so it felt like a safe place, a place of refuge even from the constant barrage of foul language in society and the constant fight in my mind. That is no longer the case, so I now must practice "living with the uncomfortable" in order not to feed the compulsions. I am not suggesting here that Christians should not use foul language. Many Christians believe it to be okay, and I am not an expert on biblical studies to know what the Bible truly teaches. My goal is to help Christians be aware that their words for or against something can negatively affect those who have Scrupulosity.

The list could go on and on. How we dress, spend our money, what we do on "the Sabbath," how long we should pray or read our Bibles, and so on can all be sources of obsessions and compulsions for those with Scrupulosity. Combined with political and social issues, an unending supply of potential targets can overwhelm and lead to more severe mental illness. My point is that those in religious authority, especially, need to be mindful of what they teach as necessary for salvation.

It is not that pastors and leaders should not address these sorts of topics, but rather a call to be mindful that a person with Scrupulosity may need a gentle reminder that they do not have to make every issue their own. It is also a reminder to those around them that just because a person is not making the same changes in their life that you do does not mean they aren't spiritual or following the guidance of the Holy Spirit. Their plate may already be full of other things they are working on.

Equally important to what is preached and discussed are those topics which are left in silence, relegated to the realm of crude jokes and uncomfortable laughter. While researching this book, it became apparent that masturbation is a major issue for many with Scrupulosity. It is not, of course, only those with Scrupulosity who find the intersection between their spirituality and this part of their lives to be a stumbling block. One college professor I spoke with relayed that in her many years of experience as both a preacher and a professor, upwards of seventy-five percent of young people who struggle in their faith do so because of this one subject, and yet, the church fails to provide guidance on this. When I say "fails to provide guidance," I am not ignorant of the fact that some church denominations have declared unequivocally that masturbation is a sin and therefore consider the discussion to be over. I want to be careful here, but I think this fails to address the why or the how.

Some individuals with Scrupulosity face an especially torturous cycle surrounding masturbation. Often the very word can trigger unwanted sexual arousal, and once the cycle of obsession starts, it becomes like any other obsessive-compulsive cycle. When this happens, the overwhelming intrusive thoughts, the building anxiety, and the repeated compulsions to try to deal with it are met with increasing arousal. As one woman told me, "I masturbate so I can get it over with, get my brain back and move on." This would be similar to other OCD cycles involving sexual desires, but when masturbation is equated with sin, an additional layer of shame is added. A person with Scrupulosity who masturbates will often consider themselves equal to a sexual pervert, or will not see how giving into their urges to masturbate is different than giving into other sexual sins. Several related that they believe masturbation is their "besetting sin," the sin they cannot overcome no matter what they do. Sadly, many will give up trying, consider themselves backslidden, and relinquish their relationship with God.

I realize this is a difficult topic, one for which I am not an expert either in the theological, psychological, or medical fields. With the obvious suffering that a hardline approach induces, however, I wonder if the church could consider the harm done by placing it in a category with other sexual sins. It would lessen the suffering if there is a place of compassion for those who want so badly to have a relationship with God but struggle in this way with the "appetites of the flesh" which are part of normal human sexuality.

A hardline approach fails to take into consideration that, like other addictive and compulsive behaviors, masturbation is a form of self-soothing. For some, masturbation may have begun as a result of the sexual abuse they suffered as children. There are many forms of self-soothing that do not receive this type of shaming. Is this really all that different from other appetites people struggle with? We do not tell a diabetic that eating a donut will send them to hell or a person who just cannot resist that second helping of mashed potatoes that they are sinful for giving into their appetites. Why is sunbathing not a sin if it does damage to the body?

For those suffering from Scrupulosity, the condemnation of masturbation as sinful only increases the shame and compulsive need to resolve the problem. Thus, the obsessive-compulsive cycle begins. My heart goes out especially to those with Scrupulosity because of how difficult the obsessive/compulsive cycle can be. I would ask for pastors and other leaders to be mindful of the consequences of a hardline approach, of adding to the burden these people already carry.

Perhaps the most significant thing that pastors, religious leaders, and Christians, in general, can do is to preach the good news of the Gospel as the good news it is. Many of us grew up only hearing about salvation as a means to avoid hell. It was not presented as the freedom to live as we were intended to live, experiencing the wonderful—but at times difficult—process of being transformed more and more into the image of Christ.

Teach that we can trust the Holy Spirit in our lives to guide us. Many of us grew up hearing Scriptures like, "The heart is deceitful above all things and desperately wicked: who can know it?" (Jeremiah 17:9 KJV). These were used to keep us off balance spiritually and dependent on religious authorities to tell us what was right and wrong. We need to hear the good news that the Holy Spirit is with us and is the One responsible for helping us grow up into maturity in Christ. We can trust that the Holy Spirit will guide us when we are being disobedient. God truly desires a relationship with us and is not going to let us go easily.

Tell us the fantastic news that the New Creation has already begun: "Therefore, if anyone is in Christ, the new creation has come: The old has gone, the new is here!" (2 Corinthians 5:17). We need to hear that God has already made us new; we were "washed...sanctified... justified in the name of the Lord Jesus

Christ and by the Spirit of our God." (1 Corinthians 6:11b). This is good news! This is the Gospel!

As part of a Christian community, we have the responsibility and the privilege of speaking hope into the lives of those suffering from Scrupulosity. Being mindful of what we say and do can help prevent adding to the burden they already carry. Trusting the presence of the Holy Spirit in the lives of others can help us guard against judging others' spirituality based on their political views. To quote John Wesley again, "Though we cannot think alike, may we not love alike?"[19] Make it so in us, Lord Jesus.

---

19. https://www.crivoice.org/cathspirit.html.

Chapter 9

Hope from a Rewritten Story

Once upon a time, so the story goes, there were six blind men who had never encountered an elephant. One day, they came across one in their travels, and they each grabbed onto a part of the elephant. The first man, falling against the elephant's side, exclaimed, "Oh, an elephant is hard like a wall!" The second man, grabbing the tail, argued, "No, an elephant is like a rope." The third man found the ivory tusk and was sure that an elephant is sharp like a sword. One by one, each of the blind men described to the others what an elephant is like based on the one small piece of the elephant he was touching. An argument broke out as each man insisted he knew from personal experience what an elephant is like. They were all of them right, but they were all of them wrong.

I sometimes feel my own story has been a bit like that. I see one part and think I understand the whole. I see my life experiences from my own perspective and forget they are just one aspect. My healing journey has revealed some of the behind-the-scenes ways God was working in my life, even when I was unaware of it.

Discovering nearly nine years ago that I have Religious Scrupulosity OCD was like a light going on in my mind. Suddenly, all the things I had struggled with for most of my life made sense. Years of counseling, while not addressing the Scrupulosity, had nevertheless produced movement toward healing and health, so having that missing puzzle piece allowed me to finally work on freeing myself from the stranglehold it had on me. Having worked on other areas of Obsessive-Compulsive Disorder in my life, I already had the tools to deal with the Scrupulosity. In a very short time of putting those into practice, I managed to begin to live more freely. When thoughts came into my mind, I learned not to try to wash them away with Scripture or song but instead let them continue floating on down the stream. When intrusive sexual thoughts about God would appear, I would take them to God and sit there in trust, assured that God knew me and loved me and understood. Gradually the intrusive thoughts became fewer and fewer as I learned not to respond to them. I have become a master at "living with the uncomfortable."

Although I was finding health and healing from the mental illness, I was still struggling with identity issues. For so long, I had been dependent on Norm, my kids, and others around me for a sense of identity. About five years ago, Dr. Diane Leclerc—premier theologian in the Church of the Nazarene and Professor at Northwest Nazarene University—was leading a Bible study at our church. She mentioned that for many years it was preached that pride is the root of all sin. She disagreed. She talked about how so many women try to "get rid of pride" when they instead suffer from low self-esteem. Pride is not their issue. She proposed that the root of all sin is instead idolatry: the idolatry of self and idolatry of others. As she continued teaching, I saw myself so clearly and was convicted that it was time to stop looking to others for my sense of identity.

It is important to note that my identity was never allowed to develop in a healthy way as a very young child. Part of my survival depended on being who I thought others wanted me to be. Attaching myself to others and taking on their identity was the only way I knew how to cope with the spiritual and emotional abuse I was enduring. I survived, not in the healthiest way, but I survived. So, in recognizing that it was time to let Christ continue developing my own personal identity, there was no shame or guilt for the ways I had survived; there was just a recognition that I did not need those anymore.

It was scary letting go of all the ways I had identified myself. It was also freeing. For the first time in my life, I experienced personhood. I began to allow myself to explore my likes and dislikes, develop opinions, and be whom God had created me to be. And I discovered that I like that person! I also began to experience joy for the first time since early childhood.

However, one area where I continued to struggle was understanding my place in this world. For most of my life, not having an identity, I did not know who I was or where I fit. I always felt that I was on the outside looking in, wanting to be a part but not knowing how to get in. It was that way with my family, church, other relationships, and especially in my relationship with God. A vague uneasiness plagued me, an uneasiness that said I did not belong.

About four years ago, an incredible woman moved to our area and began attending our church. I found out that she is a licensed spiritual director. A spiritual director is one who has been trained to listen and help people discern where God is working in their lives. I began working with Barbara and was learning to recognize God's fingerprint in my life. For about a year, I worked with her, and it was a valuable time of growth. I reached a point, though, where I became "stuck," unable to feel connected to God; that familiar feeling of being on the outside looking in was haunting me. I felt there was a core issue that I could not quite identify, keeping me from growing. Barbara suggested we try emotional healing prayer. Essentially, emotional healing prayer is praying over a specific time or memory and inviting God to speak truth into that memory. (I have been told, although I have not personally experienced it, that it is similar to what is accomplished with a psychological tool called EMPR—eye movement desensitization and reprocessing). I had been reading about emotional healing prayer myself and wondered if that might help me, so we decided to proceed.

To be honest, I did not think anything would happen. Specifically, I did not believe God would show up. I was afraid I would be embarrassed because, yet again I would be a failure at hearing from God. I was desperate for relief, though. During that first session, I came not knowing what to expect. As we settled into our chairs, closed our eyes, and had a few minutes of silence, I tried to quiet my mind and prayed that God would help me hear what He had to say to me. Barbara quietly began to pray. I was a bit surprised! I thought she would start praying for me as a young child when memories already existed. Instead, she felt led to begin praying for me as a fetus in my mother's womb. She prayed that God would take me back to that time and help me envision what it would have been like. As we prayed, I was taken back in my imagination to what it felt like to be there, safe and protected. Interestingly enough, what I also felt was sadness and lostness. Following God's prompting in her praying, Barbara asked God to show me the warmth of His presence there with me, so that I would somehow know He was there. I found myself surrounded by God's warmth and saw His hands reaching out toward me. Then, I heard His words to me: "You are wanted," they said. Three times God repeated those words, "You are wanted. You are wanted. You are wanted." Barbara continued praying, but for me, time stood still. At that moment, God rewrote my entire life story. Like one of those 3-D pictures that if you turn it just a bit, you see a different picture; I saw my whole life in a completely different way.

There were things I had never discussed with Barbara about my conception and birth. I am the youngest of eight children. After my brother, John, who is just 14 months older than I am, was born, my dad had a vasectomy, so when my mom became pregnant with me, my dad was certain my mom had had an affair. My older siblings remember the fights they had. However, a trip back to the doctor—and a second surgery!—reassured my dad that I was indeed his. About a year before she passed away, my mother told me another piece of my story. Our family was incredibly poor, and my mom was concerned they would not have the money to feed and clothe another child, so she went to her doctor and asked if he would help her with an abortion. (My mother's understanding along these lines was very limited, so I do not at all fault her for this.) Her doctor, a Christian man, explained that, in his opinion, it would be murder, so she did not pursue it further.

One final piece has to do with what modern research has discovered about how trauma, including emotional trauma, to a mother while she is pregnant can change her unborn baby's DNA, and that change can persist for three to four generations afterward, causing an increased risk for depression and other mental illnesses.[20] I'm convinced that my mom's trauma with an unexpected pregnancy, the fights with my dad, and my mom's emotional rejection of me were responsible for that "outside looking in" feeling I had experienced my entire life. I did not know those memories existed as my earliest "memories," but I had sure experienced their effects and was formed by them.

Yet, at that moment, when God spoke those words, "You are wanted!" my life changed. God rewrote my entire story. No longer was I "unwanted," but the very Creator of the universe wanted me from the moment of my conception. There was never a moment I was without the care and love of God, never a moment when I did not belong. I was not aware I needed to hear those words, but God knew and spoke the truth into those earliest memories. Words are not adequate to describe the transformation of my life since that moment. With my earlier commitment to finding my identity in Christ, and with this revelation of always being wanted, I have made great strides in becoming the unique person God created me to be. I know who I am and, more importantly, whose I am. When I gave my life to Jesus when I was four years old (one of my earliest memories), I stepped into a truth already written on my heart.

Barbara's prayer continued, though. She prayed that God would show God's presence to me throughout the ordeal of the birth process and that God would be the one who welcomed me into this world. God was faithful to that, and I experienced the warmth of God's presence and acceptance even at birth. Barbara prayed for that tiny baby as she was taken home, that I would know God was always with me. This was another

---

20. https://www.ncbi.nlm.nih.gov/pmc/articles/PMC3710585/

essential part of my story I had not shared with Barbara. When I was born, my sister had whooping cough, so my mom was not allowed to take me home with her. Instead, I went to my grandparents' house, and they had me for the entire first month of my life. Although I saw my mom a few times, she related to me how there was fear that she could pass whooping cough to me if she held me, so her physical interaction with me was very minimal.

That tiny baby, carried nine months inside her mother, listening to that heartbeat, hearing that voice, was suddenly deprived of both. Modern research is beginning to study and understand the lasting psycho-social consequences being separated from the birth mother can have on a baby.[21] Add to this that after a month of being with my grandparents, I suffered another loss when I returned home. Fear of abandonment was a huge issue I had grappled with for my entire life. As Barbara was praying, I experienced the presence of God going with me as I left the hospital to go to my grandparents' house and then again when I returned to my own house. God was there every moment. I had never been abandoned, and deep in my heart, that part of me was healed with that knowledge.

One of the most amazing results of God beginning to rewrite my story with the truth was that my social anxiety began to lessen almost immediately. My social anxiety, in part, was fueled by the belief that I was "less than" everyone else and had less value. I was often apologetic over my existence as if I did not deserve to take up time, oxygen, and space. Being able to speak up in a group or to approach someone to talk to

---

21. https://www.psychologicalscience.org/publications/observer/obsonline/how-mother-child-separation-causes-neurobiological-vulnerability-into-adulthood.html

them—especially if they were a religious leader—was nearly impossible. I would have panic attacks at the mere thought. The part of social anxiety attached to the Scrupulosity had already greatly diminished, but the warped identity part still affected me. When God rewrote that part of my story and declared me "wanted," suddenly I began to feel that I genuinely belonged; I was just as valuable and deserving of love and respect as the most important religious leader or distinguished statesperson. I was given purpose again, not for something I was doing, but simply because I was wanted and loved by God. That tiny fetus had not done a thing to earn God's love, had never prayed a sinner's prayer, had never told another person about Jesus. Before I had done anything, I was already loved and wanted by God! Nothing and nobody could change that. What an incredible and life-changing realization!

Over the following weeks, Barbara and I continued working through my childhood, pausing to pray for anything God specifically brought to mind. God spoke truth over and over into my memories, letting me see that God had been there the whole time. However, there were two particularly troublesome memories that I finally worked up the courage to bring to God. One was my dad's silent treatment.

In those early formative years of my life, my dad's silent treatment was something I dreaded and feared. I would do anything to avoid making my dad mad at me because the devastation of the silent treatment was more than I could handle. I learned to panic at the mere hint of conflict around me, becoming utterly intolerant of it. Not surprisingly, my dad's silent treatment bled over into my relationship with God. As a child, I understood God's "silence"—or my perception that God was silent—in the same way I understood my dad's silent treatment: I must have done something terrible and deserved to be punished. I wanted so badly to be loved by those around me and by God that I would become whomever I needed to be to avoid being—as I perceived—abandoned by them.

One morning I told Barbara that I wanted to do some healing prayer work around my dad's silent treatment. Barbara and I had chatted many times about the impact my dad's silent treatment had on me. We talked a bit about that, and then I shared with her how I felt it was affecting me in my day-to-day life. We then took it to God, asking God to reveal the truth in the situation and to do for me what God knew I needed.

This time, God brought to Barbara's mind the story from Scripture of Jesus crying over Jerusalem and saying how He longed to gather them as a mother hen gathers her chicks under her wings. She prayed that God would gather me into the safety of His wings, and I felt enfolded in the warmth and security of God's protection. Barbara then began praying that God would take me back in my mind to one of those times when my dad was giving me the silent treatment. She asked that God would help me see the room and myself there, then she prayed that God would help me envision my dad in the room. It was easy to place myself in my childhood home with my dad in his recliner hidden behind his newspaper. It was a familiar scene that had played out many times in my life. Barbara prayed that I would know I was not invisible, that I was not forgotten or unloved.

I thought God would speak to me as He had in the past, but this time the focus was totally on my dad. The thought struck me that Dad was hiding behind his newspaper and behind the silent treatment because he did not know what else to do. It crossed my mind that the silent treatment was not about me and my failures; it was not about my naughtiness or unacceptability. It was about my dad and his feelings of inadequacy as a parent.

While this was going on in my mind, Barbara had stopped praying for a little bit. Later, when we talked about what had happened while she was praying, she said she had been wrestling with what she felt God was telling her to pray, but she finally told God that she would pray as God was directing. God was leading her to pray that I would see my dad with compassion and see that the silent treatment was not about me; it was about his own lack of knowing what to do. She prayed that I would see that the problem was my dad's, but that I had taken it on as a problem with myself. She was praying precisely what God had already been showing me!

During our time praying, I not only saw myself safely enfolded in God's care, but I also saw my mom being cared for and protected by God. My mom had suffered the full brunt of my dad's silent treatment many times, sometimes for weeks or months at a time (3 months was the longest). I was comforted to know God was caring for my mom through all that she went through. I also saw that Jesus was standing near my dad, and I kept expecting He would go over and care for my dad's brokenness as well, but my dad kept his newspaper up, and his "walls" were almost palpable.

We prayed for a bit longer, then chatted about what God had done in me. I explained to Barbara that even before she began praying for me to realize the silent treatment was not about me but was about my dad, God had already shown me that very thing! It was pretty amazing to Barbara. She said she had never prayed that way before but felt very strongly that was how she was supposed to pray—for my dad and not so much for me. We talked about how I internalize everything as being a problem with me instead of realizing that others often act out of their own brokenness. My dad's "rejection" was not a rejection of me. My dad loved me, and I believe if he had known a different way to parent, he would have. It was the same with many people who took their brokenness out on me throughout my childhood. I realize that so much of it was not even about me. I accepted blame and guilt for stuff that had little to nothing to do with me.

When we were almost done with our time together, I remembered to tell Barbara about seeing my mom being cared for by Jesus and seeing Jesus standing near my dad. I told her I felt sad for my dad because his walls were so high that he could not receive God's embrace. Barbara made the statement, "You weren't the only one who experienced his silent treatment!"

It is hard to explain what that statement did to me, but it took my breath away. Never have I so fully understood that Jesus knows how I feel. He has experienced the awfulness of what I have experienced. That brought me to tears. The only way I can say how I felt was to say I knew myself to be standing on holy ground. Even now, writing this, the tears start. I am still incapable of putting into words what that meant to me, and how Jesus ministered to me deeply at that moment.

For others who experienced my dad's silent treatment, I think it is important to say that I do recognize my dad used the silent treatment in very manipulative destructive ways that left deep woundedness. There was a selfish—and dare I say wicked—aspect to some of the ways he used the silent treatment, and my story does not at all negate the awfulness of that. The wounds Dad caused others will need a different type of healing than what I needed, and my heart longs with theirs for that healing.

I also want my readers to know that, although I need to include some of the details of how my dad mistreated me for you to understand my story, it is also important to know that my dad and I ended up with a close and treasured relationship.

One of the most significant memories Barbara and I worked through with emotional healing prayer was an incident that had profoundly affected me and around which I had written most of the story of my life. It is the story I shared in Chapter 2 about me as a nine-year-old at a revival service. I had gone forward to pray, and my aunt had come to pray with me, "Debi, tell God you'll quit wearing pants; tell God you'll quit cutting your hair, etc." It was a devastating moment that shaped my spiritual life in negative ways. It was one of my deepest scars and memories, which I felt still held power over me.

It was with deep trepidation that I approached that time of prayer. I was again afraid that God would not have anything to say and that what I had believed about myself as a result of that time at the altar might be true. Perhaps I had so failed God back then that I deserved to suffer. Trusting God with the outcome, I told Barbara I was ready to bring this memory to God.

Inviting God to be in that moment in whatever way God saw fit, Barbara began to pray. She asked that God would take me back to that time, to that memory. Instead of praying for me already kneeling at the altar, though, Barbara felt led to pray for me as I sat on the bench hearing the sermon before the altar call. She prayed that IF God was speaking to me to go to the altar, and IF He had wanted to touch my life in a special way that night, I would know it was Him calling me. She then prayed that Jesus would accompany my little-girl self to the altar. Next, Barbara felt led to pray for protection around that little girl, that God would protect her from any voices which were not from God. She also felt led to pray the Scriptures about it being better to have a millstone hung around a person's neck than to cause one of these little ones to stumble. She prayed that while my aunt was whispering into my left ear, God would speak into my right ear. After praying for a while, she prayed that if there was anything God wanted to say to my little-girl self, He would do so. A little bit later, she ended our time of prayer together, asking God that whenever I visited that memory, it would be a memory that was filled with God's presence and truth. After that, we processed through what God had revealed to me.

As Barbara had prayed that IF God was calling me to the altar, I was immediately struck by the fact that never, in all my life since that long-ago moment, had I considered that it was not God who had called me to the altar. I had always assumed that the "conviction" I was feeling was from the Holy Spirit and that I needed to go to the altar and repent. It had not occurred to me that I had been to the altar many times (and many, many, many more after that moment!) because I thought I was feeling "conviction." What God revealed to me at that moment is that the conviction I was feeling was a result of the pressure I was under from my relatives and the conservative holiness church to conform to their standards as a way of knowing I was saved. God's words to me as we prayed—and back into that moment of time—were, "You were already mine!" God already had my heart. I was already God's child, and it was not God calling me to the altar. God showed me that I had tried to follow someone else's path. I already belonged to Godself! That was a powerful thing for me to realize.

Next, as Barbara prayed for God to protect me as I knelt at the altar, I had a picture of Jesus sticking His arm out and putting His hand straight in front of my aunt's face in a gesture that clearly told her to be quiet. I was embarrassed by this and thought that Jesus would not act that way. I was not going to tell Barbara about that because I was afraid it was my own thought, but then she said to me that as she prayed, in her own mind, she had asked God to not only protect me emotionally but, if possible, to do something *physical* which would let me know God was protecting me. That is why she had prayed about the millstone. I was reminded of Jesus telling Peter, "Get thee behind me, Satan!" Jesus had shown me that my aunt's words were not His words. Another way God protected me was revealed when Barbara prayed that while my aunt spoke into my left ear, God would speak into my right ear. Always in my memory, my aunt had spoken into my right ear. Instead of God speaking into the opposite ear, Jesus spoke into my right ear and came between my aunt and me so that her words could not reach me at all. Jesus provided another physical barrier of protection.

Finally, Barbara prayed that if God wanted to speak any truth into that moment, God would do so, and I "heard" God say, "You did not fail me." Several times God said that to me. "You did not fail me!" I cannot tell you how profoundly healing that was! I had not realized how much fear I had carried since that moment—fear that I had failed to follow God, fear that I had "put my hand to the plow and turned back," fear that I had been disobedient. All my years of doubt over my salvation could be traced back to when I left the altar feeling like I could never measure up to what God wanted, that I could never be good enough or holy enough to earn God's love. Knowing God was not disappointed in me at the altar brought healing to one of my darkest days. As I say about some of my earlier experiences with healing prayer, "God rewrote my story."

This was another step in my spiritual and emotional healing journey. I am amazed at how God ministered in such profound ways, addressing things I had not even realized were at the very heart of the problem. It is likely that throughout the rest of my life, I will continue to learn more and more about how God was always present and active in my life, even when I thought God was being silent.

I would never want to leave my readers with the impression that my journey is indicative of how God always works. I am but one individual and the ways God has reached through to me in the midst of Scrupulosity and severe identity issues are not the ways God ministers to everyone. I know well my own drive to find the right formula, the right way to pray, the right books to read, and the right sermons to listen to in order to experience God in the way I think I should. There is, however, no magic formula. Sometimes seeking God with our whole hearts looks like letting go of our need for certainty and resting in faith. Sometimes the most challenging work of saying "yes" to Jesus is trusting Him to do His job of transforming us more and more into the image of Christ.

Likewise, I would not want to leave my readers with the impression that I have arrived mentally, emotionally, or most importantly, spiritually, at total health and wholeness. My journey continues. As I write this, I am preparing to meet with my spiritual director to once again work with emotional healing prayers to probe more deeply into some areas of my life where healing has not yet taken place. I expect this process will continue throughout my life. While I have had some incredible moments of God's felt presence in my life, there are still long days of silence and the seeming absence of God. Scrupulosity, while greatly diminished, is still a reality I deal with, sometimes daily. Just because I now have the tools to deal with it does not mean it has completely gone away. I still must guard against it overtaking my life again. I am still learning how to balance asking for help from my pastors and other religious leaders when I need it with not falling back into the habit of seeking assurance in unhealthy ways. Generally, now, I err on the side of being afraid to ask for help in case it is the Scrupulosity talking. That is still an area where further growth needs to happen.

My point is that it is okay not to have everything figured out. Growth is a lifelong process, and while at times it is frustrating and even discouraging, there is also an enormous element of joy in living through the process. I used to pray for instant healing of all my mental health issues, but now I am convinced it would have deprived me of some of the most profound moments of growth in my life. My prayer for those who suffer from Scrupulosity is that they will find joy in the moments of healing and be able to see the hard work of the process of healing as a positive answer to Jesus' question, "Do you want to get well?"

One final point along those lines is that I realize my story may convey the incorrect notion that spiritual, supernatural healing is how I recovered from Scrupulosity. Much of this book has indeed focused on my spiritual healing and how God has rewritten my story. However, as indicated elsewhere, I went through many, many years of counseling, intensely working through my phobias, obsessions, depression, and anxiety. I am convinced there is no quick fix for mental illness. It requires the dailiness of putting in the time and effort to learn better coping skills, working through the effects of trauma, taking medication when appropriate, and choosing faith over feeling. Years of doing those things are what set the foundation for overcoming (and continuing to overcome) the Religious Scrupulosity OCD. It has been a difficult journey, and often it felt like I was not making any progress. Most of the time I am convinced I will struggle with some of this for the rest of my life. And that is okay! Continued growth means I am still alive and making forward progress.

Chapter 10

The Continuing Blessing of Healing

"When Esau heard his father's words, he burst out with a loud and bitter cry and said to his father, 'Bless me—me too, my father!'

But he said, 'Your brother came deceitfully and took your blessing.'

Esau said, 'Isn't he rightly named Jacob? This is the second time he has taken advantage of me: He took my birthright, and now he's taken my blessing!' Then he asked, 'Haven't you reserved any blessing for me?'

Isaac answered Esau, 'I have made him lord over you and have made all his relatives his servants, and I have sustained him with grain and new wine. So, what can I possibly do for you, my son?'

Esau said to his father, 'Do you have only one blessing, my father? Bless me too, my father!' Then Esau wept aloud. (Genesis 27:34-38)

There are few scenes in all of Scripture more tragic than this one. I cannot read it without my heart clenching with sorrow, compassion, and perhaps even some anger. Setting aside the cultural context and the part this story plays in the overarching story of redemption throughout the Bible, it seems like such an unfair and horrible story. This, I thought, was also my story. For most of my life, I had longed for "the blessing," but watched as others around me received it while I thought I was going away unblessed and empty-handed. In my mind, "the blessing" was synonymous with the felt presence of God, so in church services, as people were experiencing the presence of God while I sat there empty, I would beg God, "Bless me, too!" The sorrow over feeling like I was denied that blessing would rip me apart in my soul and pile on more shame and guilt. I pondered over and over what I could do to be worthy of that blessing, but thought that just like in the story of Esau, perhaps I would go away with nothing.

All my begging and pleading did not bring the blessing, and neither did all my scrupulous attempts to live righteously. Far from helping me see how I was misunderstanding what Scripture was talking about in the story of Esau, the church of my childhood instead heaped on more shame, verifying that I was not worthy of the blessing I so desired. In subtle ways, my relatives also let me know that I was an Esau to their Jacob.

But, the story of Jacob and Esau—and my own story—does not end with Jacob stealing the blessing and Esau going away empty-handed. That story really is not even about Jacob and Esau. The story is about how through the descendants of one, the whole earth ended up being blessed through the life, death, and resurrection of Jesus.

In the Sermon on the Mount in Matthew 5, Jesus tells us who is blessed. "Blessed are the poor in spirit; blessed are those who mourn; blessed are the meek; blessed are those who hunger and thirst for righteousness; blessed are the merciful; blessed are the pure in heart; blessed are the peacemakers; blessed are the persecuted." A number of years ago, I read in Dallas Willard's book, *The Divine Conspiracy*, that the Beatitudes are not so much a description of those who are holy, as it is an invitation to blessing for those who have nothing. As Jesus spoke to the crowd before Him, there were the poor and the needy, the persecuted and the forgotten. They were blessed not because they had already attained some level of holiness or righteousness, but because of Who stood before them. The provider of all blessings is the One offering them hope and light in the midst of their poverty of life and spirit. The way to make oneself worthy of receiving a blessing, then, is to recognize one's own dependence on Christ. It is not based on a person's ability to earn it. This is good news for those who long for God's blessing!

Over the last couple of years, I have spent a good amount of time contemplating what it means to be "in Christ." From childhood, I have heard so much about how Jesus lives in my heart, "Christ in you, the hope of glory," (Colossians 1:27b), and other Scriptures that mention Christ living in us. Those are Scriptures expressing powerful truths. However, for a person like myself who struggles with Scrupulosity, sometimes those Scriptures and the concept of Christ living in me left me frantic with anxiety to make sure I was holy enough and sinless enough for Jesus to continue to live there. (Remember that I was deeply formed by the concept that God could not dwell where there was sin.) When I think of verses about Jesus being in me, it feels like the pressure is totally on me for my spiritual life. However, Scripture puts the emphasis on what Christ does for us, and our complete dependence on Him. He is the one responsible for transforming us into His image. It is the "Fruit of the Spirit" that is growing in us, not the fruit of the individual. 2 Corinthians 5:17 says, "Therefore, if anyone is in Christ, the new creation has come: The old has gone, the new is here!" When I think about being "in Christ," I have a mental picture of myself surrounded by the vastness of God. In Christ, I am transformed. In Christ, I am safe and secure from anything which would try to come between God and me. In Christ, I can rest. In Christ, I am blessed.

Shortly after I started to experience God's rewriting of my story, I began to feel a renewed call of God on my life. I first experienced this as a child, sensing that God was "setting me apart" for some sort of ministry. I thought maybe I would be a missionary or perhaps teach biblical studies at a university. Mental illness, however, completely changed the course of my life and required most of my energy for simple survival. As God renewed the call on my life, at first, I was filled with shame, feeling like I had not been obedient to God by not "fulfilling" that call. As I prayed about it, though, God began to reveal to me that I had been obediently faithful to God throughout my life, and that I had not failed to live out my calling. God began to show me all the ways I had served in spite of being mentally ill. God reminded me how, with Norm's help, we had raised three wonderful children. Regardless of the fact that I was sometimes nearly paralyzed with the Scrupulosity, I had managed to homeschool my kids, not just because it was convenient due of all our military moves, but also because I was good at it! God brought to mind all the women I had mentored over the years, pointing them to Christ even when I wasn't sure I was saved. When Norm was in charge of a large office of mostly women, I took "Tuesday Treats" in for them, letting them know they were cared for. From that, I ended up discipling two of the women and receiving official recognition from the United States Air Force for my volunteerism and was given the Air Force Angel Award. Because my churches were places I felt secure enough to go, I spent time volunteering wherever I was needed. One of our churches awarded us the Nazarene Distinguished Service Award for our work there.

I tell about this not to glorify myself but to demonstrate the incredible faithfulness of God in my life even in the midst of my being severely mentally ill. Christ was working in and through me to fulfill God's call on my life, even when I could not see it and did not think it was happening.

A few years ago, a wonderful woman was mentoring me through a book about discovering your spiritual gifts. While I was not surprised that "teaching" was my most prominent spiritual gift, I was nonetheless chagrined by the fact that social anxiety made it almost impossible for me to teach. Speaking up in a group was hard enough without the added stress of leading the group. Yet, I do love to teach. Mentoring is certainly one way I have done that, but I am also realizing that teaching can happen other ways, such as through writing a book. I am becoming convinced that sometimes we do not have to go looking for that to which God is calling us. We just need to be faithful in the "little things."

Over these last few years since discovering I have Scrupulosity, so much in my life has changed. I am often amazed at the person I am becoming. In February, 2020, I had the opportunity to lead a workshop titled, "Obsessed with Jesus: Scrupulosity as Moral Disability," at Northwest Nazarene University's Wesley Conference. I am still astonished that I did that! Over the last few months in the process of writing this book, I have had many opportunities to educate individuals and religious leaders about Scrupulosity, and I often find myself marveling at the calmness I have experienced. Reaching out to different people while writing this book has been another demonstration of the growth I'm experiencing. I feel like I am finally finding my voice and developing my own personhood.

It is likely that I will struggle with some parts of Scrupulosity for the rest of my life. Acquiring the tools to deal with it when it is active has been an important part of my healing journey. Even more transforming, though, has been learning to rest in the truth that God sees me and knows me; I can rest in the knowledge that even when I do not have things perfectly figured out, I can trust that Jesus is doing what He said He would do, transforming me more and more into the image of Christ. I can rest, knowing I am blessed not because of who I am, but because of who Christ is. His blessing is so much more than just the "felt presence" of God I had mistakenly believed it was. It includes the ability to rest in the finished work of Christ. I am blessed, indeed!

Offering a blessing to others is a long tradition not only reflected within stories like that of Jacob and Esau but also embedded in the liturgy of various religions. In the Old Testament, part of the rituals of the Tabernacle—and later, the Temple—was this blessing found in Numbers 6:24-26: "The Lord bless you and keep you; the Lord make his face shine on you and be gracious to you; the Lord turn his face toward you and give you peace." Down through the ages, this blessing and others like it have been used at the end of religious services. While in some churches what is called the "Benediction" has instead become a closing prayer, still many churches retain the beautiful tradition of offering this priestly blessing. Unlike a prayer directed to God with eyes closed, a benediction is directed to the people and is offered with eyes open and hands upraised over

The Continuing Blessing of Healing

the people, with the people eagerly holding out their hands to receive the blessing offered on behalf of God. It is no wonder that this part of the service has become one of my favorites.

As I bring this book to a close, I can think of no better way to end it than with a blessing. One of the great privileges we as believers have is to extend the blessings of God to others. I am sure there are many who, like me, are desperately searching for some blessing from God, not realizing that their poverty of spirit is the very thing necessary for God's blessing to be given. We have the incredible privilege of extending that blessing of hope that the presence of Jesus brings, and helping people see they are not outside God's blessing.

For those of you who read this book to learn how to help those around you struggling with Scrupulosity or an over-active conscience, I offer this blessing: May you know, yourself, the love of Christ and the peace He brings, and may you be given the wisdom to see and come alongside those who suffer. May you be filled with compassion and may the hope you have in Christ be a beacon to help light the way for others.

For those who have seen yourself and your struggles in these pages, I offer this blessing: May you know yourself to be deeply loved by God, and may you find the courage to rest in Him. May you be comforted and encouraged through your journey toward healing, knowing others see you, walk alongside you, and are holding onto faith for you in those moments when you do not seem to have faith of your own.

I have been blessed to be able to share my journey with you, my dear readers. As I have written this book, I have thought of many of you who have helped me on my journey. While I did not name many people in these pages, you are still there and appreciated more deeply than I can express. For those who so graciously shared your own stories and the stories of those you love with me, you were held gently in my heart throughout this book. I hope as we have been united in our struggles, we will also be united in finding healing and offering hope to others.

> "The Lord bless you and keep you;
> the Lord make his face shine on you and
> be gracious to you;
> the Lord turn his face toward you
> and give you peace."
> (Numbers 6:24-26)

Appendix

Additional Resources

- https://iocdf.org/faith-ocd/

    The International OCD Foundation has a page of resources dedicated to the intersection between faith and OCD. In addition, they offer a yearly "Faith and OCD Conference" for faith leaders, mental health professionals, individuals who have OCD, and their families.

- *Trauma In the Pews: The Impact on Faith and Spiritual Practices*, Janyne McConnaughey, PhD. For spiritual leaders, Trauma in the Pews is a practical and compassionate roadmap to effectively minister to those struggling with the effects of trauma. For those impacted by trauma, it will provide a path to authentic healing and a deeper connection with God.

- *Scrupulosity: A cognitive–behavioral analysis and implications for treatment Journal of Obsessive-Compulsive and Related Disorders*
    file:///C:/Users/norpe/Downloads/Scrupulosity-model-2014.pdf
    Jonathan S. Abramowitz n, Ryan J. Jacoby

University of North Carolina at Chapel Hill, Campus Box 3270 (Davie Hall), Chapel Hill, NC 27599, United States

This journal article was especially helpful in understanding Religious Scrupulosity OCD.

- *Getting Over OCD: A 10-Step Workbook for Taking Back Your Life (The Guilford Self-Help Workbook Series) Second Edition* , Dr. Jonathan S Abramowitz, (2018) The Guilford Press.

  Dr. Abramowitz is a leading researcher of OCD and Scrupulosity. He has done extensive research and has an ever-growing list of articles and journal entries in addition to his book, *Getting Over OCD*. His research was instrumental in helping me understand my own Scrupulosity OCD as well as in more fully understanding some of the challenges other suffers face. I recommend his works for mental health professionals who wish to understand Scrupulosity better. In addition, he developed the following:

- *The Penn Inventory of Scrupulosity (PIOS)-Revised* https://earlatvanderbilt.files.wordpress.com/2017/01/pios-r.doc

  The PIOS-Revised is a questionnaire devised to help identify Scrupulosity. Please seek the help and advice of a mental health professional in understanding results and pursuing treatment.

- https://therapyinanutshell.com/about/

  This website features a list of resources from a licensed therapist. She has free resources as well as ones with a cost. In addition, there are a number of YouTube videos from Therapy in a Nutshell. Again, with all resources listed here, seek the advice and help of a mental health professional for diagnosis and treatment.

References

8176.SHAR. Strong's Hebrew: 8176. רָעַשׁ (Shaar)—to calculate, reckon. (n.d.). Retrieved November 15, 2022, from https://biblehub.com/hebrew/8176.htm

Abramowitz, J. S., & Jacoby, R. J. (2014, February 4). *Scrupulosity: A cognitive-behavioral analysis and implications for treatment.* Journal of Obsessive-Compulsive and Related Disorders. Retrieved November 15, 2022, from https://www.sciencedirect.com/science/article/pii/S2211364914000116

Berle, D., & Starcevic, V. V. (2005). *Thought-action fusion: Review of the literature and Future Directions.* Clinical psychology review. Retrieved November 15, 2022, from https://pubmed.ncbi.nlm.nih.gov/15792850/

Ennulat, D. (2014, July 8). *OCD scrupulosity: Spiritual direction through the stages of recovery.* OCD Massachusetts. Retrieved November 15, 2022, from https://www.ocdmassachusetts.org/2014/06/25/ocd-scrupulosity-spiritual-direction-through-the-stages-of-recovery/

Gersema, E. (2016, December 23). *Hard-Wired: The Brain's circuitry for political belief.* ScienceDaily. Retrieved November 15, 2022, from https://www.sciencedaily.com/releases/2016/12/161223115757.htm (As cited originally in Kaplan, J., Gimbel, S. & Harris, S. Neural correlates of maintaining one's political beliefs in the face of counterevidence. Sci Rep 6, 39589 (2016). https://doi.org/10.1038/srep39589)

How mother-child separation causes neurobiological vulnerability into adulthood. Association for Psychological Science - APS. (2018, June 20). Retrieved November 15, 2022, from https://www.psychologicalscience.org/publications/observer/obsonline/how-mother-child-separation-causes-neurobiological-vulnerability-into-adulthood.html

Kaplan, J. T., Gimbel, S. I., & Harris, S. (2016, December 23). *Neural correlates of maintaining one's political beliefs in the face of counterevidence.* Nature News. Retrieved November 15, 2022, from https://www.nature.com/articles/srep39589

Kinsella, M. T., & Monk, C. (2009, September). *Impact of maternal stress, depression and anxiety on fetal neurobehavioral development.* Clinical obstetrics and gynecology. Retrieved November 15, 2022, from https://www.ncbi.nlm.nih.gov/pmc/articles/PMC3710585/

Lebowitz, E. R., Panza, K. E., & Bloch, M. H. (2015, December 22). *Family accommodation in obsessive-compulsive and anxiety disorders: A five-year update.* Expert review of neurotherapeutics. Retrieved November 15, 2022, from https://www.ncbi.nlm.nih.gov/pmc/articles/PMC4895189/

Mayo Clinic Staff. (2017, November 18). *Agoraphobia.* Mayo Clinic. Retrieved November 15, 2022, from https://www.mayoclinic.org/diseases-conditions/agoraphobia/symptoms-causes/syc-20355987

Pollard, C. A. (2010). *What is scrupulosity? - international OCD foundation.* IOCDF.org. Retrieved November 15, 2022, from https://iocdf.org/wp-content/uploads/2014/10/IOCDF-Scrupulosity-Fact-Sheet.pdf

Valentiner, D. P., & Smith, S. A. (2008, January 26). *Believing that intrusive thoughts can be immoral moderates the relationship between obsessions and compulsions for shame-prone individuals - cognitive therapy and research.* SpringerLink. Retrieved

November 15, 2022, from https://link.springer.com/article/10.1007/s10608-007-9179-1

Van Noppen, B. L. (n.d.). *Families and OCD*. International OCD Foundation. Retrieved November 15, 2022, from https://iocdf.org/families/

Wesley, J. (2018). *A Catholic spirit*. John Wesley's "On A Catholic Spirit" in Modern English. Retrieved November 15, 2022, from https://www.crivoice.org/cathspirit.html

Wilcock, P. (2000). Chapter IV The Poor In Spirit. In *The Hawk and the Dove* (pp. 253–253), Crossway Books.

Debra "Debi" Peck writes from the depth of her lived experience. Her life as a wife, mother, and grandmother is a testimony to her determination, faith, and desire to help others. When she is not writing, she enjoys quilting, reading, and solving word puzzles. Debra lives in Nampa, Idaho with her husband, Norman, and their two long-coat German Shepherds, Cali and JoJo.

ALSO FROM
SacraSage Press...

SACRASAGEPRESS.COM

ALSO FROM
SacraSage Press...

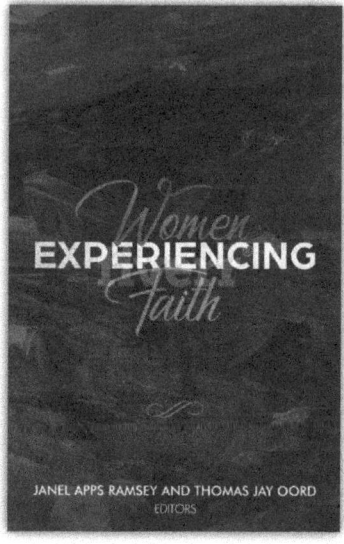

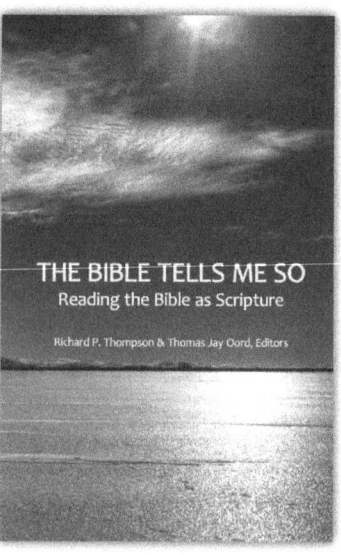

SACRASAGEPRESS.COM